The Road to YORKTOWN

The Road to YORKTOWN

JEFFERSON, LAFAYETTE AND THE BRITISH INVASION OF VIRGINIA

JOHN R. MAASS

THE
History
PRESS

Published by The History Press
Charleston, SC 29403
www.historypress.net

Front cover, top: Special Collections, John D. Rockefeller Jr. Library. *Courtesy of the Colonial Williamsburg Foundation*; *bottom*: *Advance of the Enemy*, Alfred Wordsworth Thompson. *Courtesy of the Connecticut Historical Society*.
Back cover, top: Special Collections, John D. Rockefeller Jr. Library. *Courtesy of the Colonial Williamsburg Foundation*.

First published 2015

Manufactured in the United States

ISBN 978.1.62619.391.8

Library of Congress Control Number: 2015939138

Notice: The information in this book is true and complete to the best of our knowledge. It is offered without guarantee on the part of the author or The History Press. The author and The History Press disclaim all liability in connection with the use of this book.

This book is dedicated to the many history teachers I have had over the years, particularly Carrie Irvine, J. Holt Merchant Jr., Robert M. Calhoon, Karl A. Schleunes, Mark Grimsley, Alan Gallay, Saul Cornell and John L. Brooke.

CONTENTS

ACKNOWLEDGEMENTS

Many people helped me to research, write and publish this study of the Revolutionary War in Virginia. I would like to thank Jill Bascomb, J. Temple Bayliss, Anna Berkes, Julie Bushong, Ellen M. Clark, Jimmy Clark, Ed Dandar, Patrick and Cynthia Drury, John Ferling, Benjamin P. Ford, Sarah G. Forgey, Erik Goldstein, Erin Greenwald, Joan M. Halford, Lauren A. Hammersen, Bryan J. Hockensmith, Keith Longiotti, Jane Marra, Marianne Martin, Marian McCabe, J. Britt McCarley, Nancy Moore, James Mullins, Frank O'Reilly, Todd Post, Doug Price, Thomas Reinhart, Joseph A. Seymour, Phyllis Silber, W. Scott Smith, Banks Smither, Octavia N. Starbuck, Latif A. Tarik, James Tobias, Julia Turner, Bruce Venter, William Welsch, C. James Williams III, Glenn F. Williams and Barbara Willis.

INTRODUCTION

In the spring and summer of 1781, Virginia was invaded by formidable British naval and land forces sailing from New York and marching from the Carolinas. Several times enemy troops had previously rampaged through the eastern part of the state during the American War of Independence, but this latest offensive was the most powerful and concentrated effort by the British high command to subdue the Old Dominion, ruin its military resources and prevent the state from providing desperately needed soldiers and supplies to Continental forces farther south. Led by Lieutenant General Charles Cornwallis, 2nd Earl Cornwallis, thousands of redcoats, Hessian troops and Loyalists marched, looted and burned their way across Tidewater and Piedmont Virginia, from Norfolk to Charlottesville and from the North Anna River to the Southside, followed by runaway slaves who added to the widespread destruction.

Many of the American Revolution's most well-known Patriots struggled to meet the threat of Cornwallis's incursion into Virginia. George Washington, Thomas Jefferson, Patrick Henry, the Marquis de Lafayette, "Mad" Anthony Wayne, Baron von Steuben, Nathanael Greene, Thomas Nelson Jr. and others were actively involved in the campaign to thwart the enemy's depredations east of the Blue Ridge Mountains. Continental and militia troops amassed to defend the commonwealth, some from as far away as New York and Pennsylvania. Only by concentrating troops under Major General the Marquis de Lafayette were American forces able to manage some resistance to British operations, but they were not able to prevent most of the destruction perpetrated by the enemy. Inadequate resources, too few troops and a lack of organization doomed Virginia's defensive efforts. By mid-August, Cornwallis's men had moved to a new position at Yorktown, where his Virginia expedition would eventually come to grief.

With few exceptions, most studies of the Yorktown campaign and the Revolutionary War in the South, along with biographies of key political leaders and soldiers, ignore the initial 1781 campaign in Virginia between Cornwallis and Lafayette, mention it in the broadest of terms in a few paragraphs or contain significant factual errors. Additionally, almost all of the contemporary and modern maps prepared to illustrate the widespread movements of the armies during these operations include some inaccuracies. The lack of interest in the campaign is surprising, given that Cornwallis initially expected that a successful attempt to conquer Virginia might have ended the war and the British deployed a large part of their troops, ships and resources for these operations. Moreover, this was the young Lafayette's major independent command while serving in the Continental Army in the cause for American independence, and it highlights his unusually mature military abilities as no other campaign does.

This study of the contest between Lafayette's small army, supported with difficulty by Jefferson's gubernatorial administration, and the veteran forces of Lord Cornwallis seeks to fill in the historical gap by detailing the campaign immediately preceding the Siege of Yorktown. These operations and the eventual British surrender on October 19, 1781, provide a dramatic narrative of bold maneuvers, Fabian tactics and risky strategies on both sides as the invader sought to destroy Virginia's ability to wage war and Lafayette's army while Lafayette desperately tried to avoid a defeat and maintain the American cause in the field. With a mix of daring and prudence, the French nobleman turned Continental general eventually prevailed.

1

"A SUCCESSFUL BATTLE MAY GIVE US AMERICA"

Lord Cornwallis Invades Virginia

Farewell to treaties. Fortune lead me on;
War is our judge, and in the fates our trust.
—Lucan, "Caesar Crosses the Rubicon," Pharsalia, *circa AD 61*

From his army's camp near Wilmington, North Carolina, on April 10, 1781, British lieutenant general Charles, Lord Cornwallis wrote to his superior officer at New York, General Sir Henry Clinton, to describe his uncertain situation. Several weeks earlier, his forces had defeated an American army under Major General Nathanael Greene at Guilford Courthouse, North Carolina, but at great cost. Cornwallis's army suffered casualties of over 25 percent of its strength and was unable to pursue Greene's orderly retreat after the hard-fought battle. "The fatigue of the troops and the great number of wounded put it out of my power to pursue" the enemy, Cornwallis reported, "and the want of provisions and all kinds of necessaries for the soldiers made it equally impossible to follow the blow next day." After remaining two days at Guilford, Cornwallis began to march his battered army southward toward the Atlantic coast, his soldiers "worn down with fatigue," a third of them "sick & wounded."[1]

The weary British troops marched down the Cape Fear River to Wilmington, occupied by British troops since January 1781. There, with about 1,700 redcoats, Hessians and Loyalists, Cornwallis was "employed in disposing of the sick and wounded, and in procuring supplies of all kinds, to put the troops into a proper

Lieutenant General Charles, Lord Cornwallis. *Library of Congress.*

state to take the field." With easier access to resupply at the port town, he now hoped for reinforcements in order to "enable me either to act offensively" or to move back into the interior of the state to suppress the American rebels and to "preserve the troops" from the fevers of the coastal South.[2]

Cornwallis and his battered army had been actively campaigning in the backcountry of the Carolinas since the summer of 1780, far removed from supplies and easy communications with General Clinton in New York and London authorities. After routing a larger American force at Camden, South Carolina, on August 16, 1780, his troops had pushed into western North Carolina in late January 1781. Although detachments of his army had suffered stinging defeats along the way in South Carolina at Kings Mountain (October 7, 1780) and Cowpens (January 17, 1781), Cornwallis tenaciously pursued his foe until he won a Pyrrhic victory on March 15 at Guildford Courthouse. Now at Wilmington, Cornwallis began to make new plans for his army. "I am very anxious to receive your Excellency's commands," he wrote to Clinton, "being as yet totally in the dark, as to the intended operations of the Summer."[3]

Although Cornwallis was unsure of Clinton's operational intentions, he was too experienced in military matters not to have thought about a future course of action that spring. Born in 1738 and educated at Eton, he had entered the British army's elite Grenadier Guards in 1756 and served in Europe during the Seven Years' War (1756–63) before entering the House of Lords in 1762. After the war

General Sir Henry Clinton, British commander in chief in America, 1782. *Library of Congress.*

for American independence broke out, Cornwallis began his service in the rebellious colonies in 1776 and fought at the Battles of Long Island, Brandywine, Germantown and Monmouth Courthouse and at the Siege of Charles Town, South Carolina. He obtained the rank of lieutenant general in late 1777. Lafayette later declared him "the only gentleman to have commanded the British in America." Cornwallis's victory at Camden over Major General Horatio Gates seemed to herald the beginning of a triumphant campaign to conquer the South, but by the time he reached Wilmington eight months later, success had eluded him.[4]

Cornwallis's relationship with Clinton had become strained during the 1780 Siege of Charles Town to the point that he offered little advice or support to his commander. Cornwallis, according to one modern historian, was "headstrong, impatient of the ideas of others and uncritical of his own." For much of the first several months of 1781, he sent no word at all to Clinton while marching about the Carolinas so that from January to May, his commander in New York knew little of his operations or plans.[5]

Once he arrived at Wilmington, however, Cornwallis resumed communications with New York. Continuing his April 10 letter to Clinton, Cornwallis hoped that "the Chesapeake may become the Seat of War, even (if necessary) at the expence of abandoning New York," the main British base in the rebellious colonies. He supposed that Virginia had to be brought under British control since it was the primary source of recruits and provisions for American forces in the Carolinas and Georgia. "Until Virginia is in a manner subdued," he concluded, "our hold of the Carolinas must be difficult, if not precarious."[6] Only by conquering Virginia would the rest of the South be subjugated by the king's forces, he firmly believed. Moreover, a week later, he reported directly to London that support from North Carolina's Loyalists was "passive" and that "their numbers are not so great as had been represented." Combined with the difficulty of campaigning in a province filled with hostile Patriots, difficult terrain and few provisions, Cornwallis decided against "a direct attack upon it." Summing up his position on April 18 to Lord George Germain, the British secretary of state for the colonies, Cornwallis wrote that if Great Britain wished to keep control of the territory it already possessed in the North and "to push the War in the Southern provinces," then "a serious attempt upon Virginia would be the most solid plan, because successful operations might not only be attended with important consequences there, but would tend to the security of South Carolina, & ultimately to the submission of North Carolina."[7]

The following week Cornwallis wrote again to Clinton about his preparations, not having heard from his commander at New York by the twenty-third. He reported that although his men were not yet ready to move, he would begin his advance the next day. He found it "very disagreeable to me to decide upon measures so very important and of such consequence to the general conduct of the war, without an opportunity of procuring your Excellency's directions or approbation; but the delay and difficulty of conveying letters and the impossibility of waiting for answers render it indispensably necessary." Cornwallis had received reports that in Tidewater Virginia, a British detachment under Major General William Phillips was operating "with a considerable force, with instructions to co-operate with this Army & to put himself under my orders." This news further solidified his notion that a campaign in eastern Virginia was most advantageous.[8]

Phillips's troops in Virginia included those commanded by Brigadier General Benedict Arnold, now a redcoat officer, having defected from Continental service in 1780 after a failed conspiracy to betray the Patriot defenses at West Point, New York, to the British. Arnold had been in Virginia since late December 1780 and had recently taken up a fortified position at Portsmouth. Although some historians have claimed that British officers serving with Arnold regarded him contemptuously for his treason, Phillips had nothing but praise for him. He described Arnold as an officer "whose cheerful intelligence and active zeal cannot be too much commended. I have, indeed, found in him everything I could have wished to meet in an able second."[9]

Lord Cornwallis knew that the American forces under General Greene had moved into South Carolina after the battle at Guilford Courthouse,

Benedict Arnold, the former American general who treasonously joined the British in 1780. *Library of Congress*.

and that British posts in the backcountry of that province were threatened by the Patriots. Still, Cornwallis elected to move his soldiers to Virginia, citing "the want of forage and subsistence" in South Carolina, "the almost universal spirit of revolt which prevails in South Carolina, and the strength of Greene's Army." The British commander "resolved to take advantage of General Greene's having left the back part of Virginia open and march immediately into that province, to attempt a junction with General Phillips."[10] Cornwallis hoped that if he transferred his force from Wilmington to Virginia, "a successful battle may give us America."[11] Thus, on April 24, he wrote to Phillips that he would soon join him at Petersburg, Virginia, hoping to draw Greene out of South Carolina in the process.[12]

In New York, General Clinton was unsure of Cornwallis's plans or location. He wrote to Cornwallis on April 13 that he "should continue to conduct operations as they advance Northerly," but he did not plan to send more troops to the South.[13] However, Clinton wrote this letter before receiving Cornwallis's messages from Wilmington. He was under the assumption that Greene's army had been destroyed in North Carolina and that the lower South had been pacified. Once apprised of the incomplete victory at Guilford Courthouse, Clinton began to see things differently and to doubt the wisdom of a Virginia campaign when both Carolinas were not yet pacified. Clinton wrote that Cornwallis's movement to Wilmington "has considerably changed the complexion of our affairs to the southward, and all operations to the northward must probably give place to those in favor of his Lordship, which at present appears to require our more immediate attention." In late April, he was planning to have Phillips march south to assist Cornwallis, unaware that Cornwallis was soon to meet Phillips in Virginia instead.[14]

Clinton finally began to receive more accurate intelligence from North Carolina by the end of the month. He advised Cornwallis to finish the subjugation of the Carolinas with Phillips's assistance. Clinton feared that any attempt by Cornwallis to conquer Virginia would require too much time and "might not be quite so expedient at this advanced season of the year to enter into a long operation in that climate." He also expected that once the Carolinas were under British control, Cornwallis would send most of his own force back to New York, not move to Virginia. "Had it been possible for your Lordship in your letter to me of [April] 10th...to have intimated the probability of your intention to form a junction with General Phillips," Clinton later admonished Cornwallis, "I should certainly have endeavored to have stopped you, as I did then, as well as now, consider such a move as likely to be dangerous to our interests in the Southern Colonies." Thus, when Cornwallis's refreshed troops headed north for Petersburg, he and Clinton were at odds over plans for summer operations—in particular, where they should be conducted. "My wonder at this move," wrote Clinton, "will never cease. But he has made it, and we shall say no more but make the best of it."[15]

Cornwallis left Wilmington on April 25 with an army of just over 1,400 men. His force consisted of battle-tested infantrymen of the Twenty-third, Thirty-third and Seventy-first Regiments and a small light company from the Eighty-second Regiment, which had been part of the Wilmington garrison. He had additional redcoats in his ranks under Brigadier General Charles O'Hara's Brigade of Guards, an amalgamation of soldiers drawn from the three British Regiments of Foot Guards, which had been severely bloodied at Guilford Courthouse. The Hessian Regiment von Bose and a company of light troops from the North Carolina Volunteers, a Loyalist unit, made the long trek to Virginia as well. Perhaps Cornwallis's most valuable unit on the

Lieutenant Colonel Banastre Tarleton, Cornwallis's bold cavalry leader in the South. *Library of Congress*.

march was the British Legion, a mixed formation of dragoons and infantry commanded by the hard-hitting, impetuous Lieutenant Colonel Banastre Tarleton. The legion had earned a reputation under its young colonel's leadership as a fearsome enemy force to soldiers and civilians alike.[16]

Cornwallis marched on a road skirting the many rivers, swamps and creeks of eastern North Carolina to Halifax, where Tarleton's troopers defeated a force of local militia on May 11. Soon thereafter, the British entered Virginia and crossed the Meherrin River at Hick's Ford. General Arnold had sent cavalry under Lieutenant Colonel John Graves Simcoe from Petersburg to meet Cornwallis's advancing troops. Along with Simcoe, Arnold sent a letter for Cornwallis in cipher, informing him that Phillips intended to wait at Petersburg for "five or six days in expectation of having

Blandford Church, near Petersburg, is where Major General William Phillips was buried. *Library of Congress.*

your Lordship's orders." Simcoe's detachment crossed the Nottaway River about four miles south of Stony Creek on May 11, 1781, to meet Cornwallis, whose own troops soon crossed the Nottaway there as well. His troops reached Petersburg on the morning of May 20.[17]

Although most histories of the 1781 campaign state that only upon reaching Petersburg did Cornwallis learn that General Phillips had died a week earlier of a fever, Arnold had written to the British commander on May 16 with the unwelcome news of Phillips's death. Phillips had already been secretly buried at night in an unmarked grave in the nearby cemetery of Blandford Church. He was an officer "equally loved and respected for his virtues and Military talents," noted Tarleton in his memoirs. Arnold, who succeeded Phillips in command of the troops at Petersburg, wrote similarly that the deceased general was "universally beloved and esteemed by the army,"[18] and one of Phillips's Hessian subordinates described him as "a skillfull [*sic*] and industrious officer" and "the most pleasant, unselfish, and courteous man in the world."[19]

At Petersburg, Cornwallis received recent intelligence of American and French military movements from Arnold and from Clinton's prior dispatches to Phillips, including news of French naval operations on the coast and the arrival in Virginia of a small corps of Continental soldiers under the young French nobleman Gilbet du Mortier, Marquis de Lafayette. "I will endeavor to make the best use in my power of the Troops under my command," Cornwallis assured Clinton on May 20. How Cornwallis used his troops, along with Phillips's 3,500 soldiers, in operations against Continental and Virginia troops is part of the story of the Virginia Campaign of 1781, which ultimately led to the British taking up a post in September at a small tobacco port called Yorktown.[20]

"WITH FIRE AND EVERY OTHER CRUELTY"

The British Ravage the Tidewater

And they utterly destroyed all that was in the city, both man and woman, young and old, and ox, and sheep, and ass, with the edge of the sword.
—Book of Joshua, 6:21

Lord Cornwallis's invasion of Virginia in the late spring of 1781 was not the first time the enemy had disturbed the state during the Revolutionary War. From 1779 to the end of the fighting in 1781, Virginia suffered British occupations, raids and widespread destruction of homes, warehouses, private property and military supplies. The ability of state forces to prevent the depredations of the enemy's troops was limited, as Virginia struggled to put men in the field; properly arm, train and equip them; and bring them to battle against a superior foe. By the time the enemy forces of Generals Cornwallis, Phillips and Arnold united at Petersburg in May 1781, the state was already worn out from its exertions, ravaged by the British and disorganized by its own chaotic mode of waging war.

After the last royal governor and British forces left the state in early 1776, Virginians did not feel the sting of war for several years, other than sporadic Royal Navy raids and landing parties searching for food, fresh water and plunder along the new state's coast and estuaries. The situation changed dramatically when a fleet commanded by Commodore Sir George Collier entered the Chesapeake Bay on May 8, 1779, and anchored the following day off Willoughby Point near Norfolk at the entrance to Hampton Roads.

Collier was the temporary commander of British naval forces in America until the new appointee, Vice Admiral Marriot Arbuthnot, arrived in Mid-Atlantic waters. On board Collier's transport ships were 1,800 British troops under Major General Edward Mathew. On May 10, Collier and Mathew captured Portsmouth, across the Elizabeth River from Norfolk, along with the nearby Gosport shipyard, one of the finest in America. The British secured or burned over 140 ships there and destroyed hundreds of tobacco hogsheads stacked on local quays. Kemp's Landing (now Kempsville), east of Norfolk on the Lynnhaven River, was also attacked by British troops, and Suffolk suffered heavy damages to private property and military stores as well. In the words of the Virginia Assembly, the enemy was waging war "with fire and every other cruelty unknown to civilized nations by custom or law."[21]

During this alarm, Virginia governor Patrick Henry, nearing the end of his third term in office, mobilized the militia of the Tidewater region but not until May 14. For this delay, he was loudly criticized, although in his defense, news of the British depredations around Norfolk was slow to reach him at Williamsburg, Virginia's capital. About two thousand militia responded to Henry's call to arms, but these men were poorly armed and no match for the enemy's professional troops. "Never was a country in a more shabby situation," wrote St. George Tucker, a Williamsburg lawyer and merchant who lamented that Virginia had no proper military force to "give the smallest check to an approaching enemy." The British departed Chesapeake Bay on May 24 and took with them captured military supplies, Tory supporters, prize ships and hundreds of runaway slaves. Property that could not be loaded onto British vessels was burned. The British committed "ravages and enormities, unjustified by the usage of civilized nations," Thomas Jefferson wrote bitterly to Congress. The damage was so great that Virginia's outraged legislature called on the Continental Congress to authorize attacking and burning British cities in retaliation. War had truly reached Virginia after years of not seeing the enemy.[22]

Soon after the British raiders sailed into the Atlantic, the assembly elected Jefferson as Virginia's second state governor.[23] It would be the beginning of two years of trying times for the author of the Declaration of Independence, a period of difficulties and humiliations he would soon come to lament.

Although Commodore Collier and his fleet did not stay long in Virginia, the commonwealth had not seen the last of marauding enemy forces. When news of British summer victories in South Carolina reached General Clinton at New York in 1780, he ordered an expedition to the Chesapeake

Thomas Jefferson, Virginia's
governor in 1781, by St. Memin.
Library of Congress.

Patrick Henry. *Library of Congress.*

Bay to divert the focus of southern Patriot leaders and to take pressure off Cornwallis's army in South Carolina. Clinton wanted Major General Alexander Leslie to establish a post at Portsmouth in order to raid important rebel logistical centers in the Chesapeake region and to interdict rebel supply routes to the Carolinas. Clinton had chosen an experienced officer. Leslie had been a soldier since 1753 and fought in several major battles of the Revolutionary War. After the 1780 Siege of Charles Town, he returned to New York with Clinton and commanded the elite British light infantry and grenadier battalions.[24]

Leslie's force of 2,500 men entered the Chesapeake Bay on October 20, transported by a fleet of over fifty ships. The troops landed at Portsmouth and had spread out in detachments on the north bank of the James at Newport News and Hampton by October 23. Near Portsmouth, British troops occupied Kemp's Landing and Great Bridge, and some redcoats raided as far west as Smithfield. Leslie was cautious during the raid, as he was wary of meeting Virginia militia in the field and could find few knowledgeable Tories to act as guides.[25]

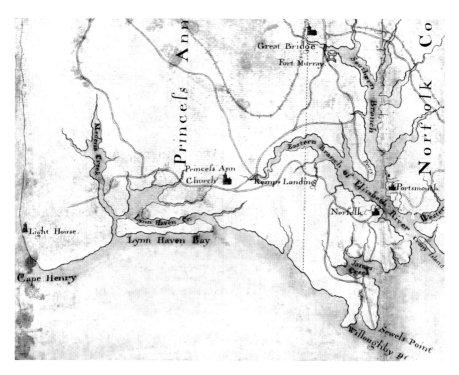

Map of eastern Virginia in 1775, with north on bottom of map. *Library of Congress.*

Governor Jefferson had called out thousands of the Tidewater-area militia to counter the British raid. Some were to gather south of the James at Smithfield under Brigadier General George Weedon, a former Continental Army general, and Brigadier General Gabriel Muhlenberg, an ordained Lutheran minister turned Continental Army military officer. On the peninsula west of Newport News, more militia gathered under the command of Thomas Nelson Jr., a prominent militia general from Yorktown and a signer of the Declaration of Independence. Unfortunately, few Virginians answered the call to muster. "The militia have appeared in such small detachments," Nelson reported to Weedon, "that it has been impossible to make any proper arrangements."[26]

Jefferson, too, had little praise for these troops, whose "function seems to have been interpreted as that of standing by and observing, rather than offering active resistance." The militia came primarily from the Tidewater counties poorly armed and equipped, and most had seen no prior military service. "The want of arms," Jefferson advised Congress, "prevents every hope of effectual opposition."[27]

Soon, Leslie received orders from Cornwallis to bring all his forces to Charles Town, South Carolina. The American victory at Kings Mountain on October 7 had cost Cornwallis 1,500 men, whom Leslie's troops would now replace. The British abandoned Portsmouth and all other Virginia posts on November 15, to the surprise of Jefferson and other Virginia leaders, and by the twenty-fourth, their ships were gone from the bay. Leslie's raid showed Jefferson and other state officials the inadequacies of Virginia's ability "for making effective opposition wherever the enemy may think proper to show themselves." Unfortunately, little could be done to shore up the state's military preparedness before the next enemy incursion into the Commonwealth, just five weeks later.[28]

On December 30, 1780, another British flotilla with 1,500 troops commanded by Benedict Arnold arrived in Virginia's Chesapeake Bay. The former Continental general was ordered by Clinton to resume the supply interdiction operations that Leslie had abandoned to reinforce Cornwallis. Arnold's command included several provincial units of Loyalists, including the Queen's Rangers under Colonel Simcoe. His detachment also included Hessian jaegers (light troops) and redcoats of the Eightieth Regiment of Foot under Lieutenant Colonel Thomas Dundas. Simcoe and Dundas were ordered by Clinton to act as Arnold's advisors during the campaign, and Arnold was to take no unnecessary risks during his stay in Virginia.[29]

The Queen's Rangers, an American Loyalist unit led by Lieutenant Colonel John G. Simcoe. *Courtesy of Colonial Williamsburg Foundation.*

Virginia authorities were caught by surprise at Arnold's sudden appearance. The enemy fleet of twenty-seven vessels observed in New York by Continental spies was assumed by Washington and others to be bound for South Carolina, in support of Cornwallis's operations. Jefferson had little firm intelligence that the British flotilla would come to Virginia, and reports sent by Washington arrived too late—he did not write to Jefferson about the enemy fleet's departure from New York on December 22 until eleven days after the British ships had sailed. Upon receiving word of warships sighted in the bay, Jefferson delayed two days before mobilizing the militia, as the identity of the vessels was not immediately known and the governor did not want to alarm and disturb the militia unnecessarily. By the time Virginians began to muster for the state's defense in early January, Arnold's fleet was already at James Town, aided by favorable winds for sailing rapidly up the James River.[30]

Virginians along the James and its tributaries panicked, abandoned their homes and fled from the enemy in an atmosphere of chaos and confusion. Jefferson wrote that "every effort was therefore necessary to withdraw the arms and other military stores, records, etc." from Richmond. The governor and state officials tried frantically to move what they could over the James River to Manchester and were particularly desperate to remove equipment from the important arms foundry at Westham, several miles

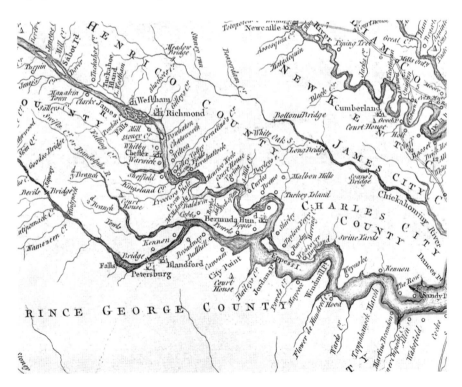

Detail of period map showing area of operations along the James River. *North Carolina Collection, University of North Carolina–Chapel Hill.*

upriver from Richmond. Jefferson personally supervised some of these efforts at the site, "giving directions about the Public Property." Due to the enemy's expected approach, some of the arms and cannons were thrown into the James River but were later recovered. Despite these precautions, "no opposition was in readiness," and Virginians were unable to halt Arnold's fast-moving foray.[31]

On January 4, 1781, Arnold landed a force of about eight hundred to one thousand men on the north bank of the James at Westover, a plantation owned by the Byrd family since the 1680s that included a stately Georgian house built in the 1750s. Arnold's men marched northwest to Richmond, where he arrived on January 5. Here and at Westham, the British destroyed small arms, four thousand French-made musket locks, canvass, rope, hemp, fuses, shot, tobacco and "a foundry for casting iron cannon," along with private property. British records indicate that twenty-four six-pounders and four iron four-pounders were spiked and damaged at Westham, as well as over three hundred barrels of powder, 1,800

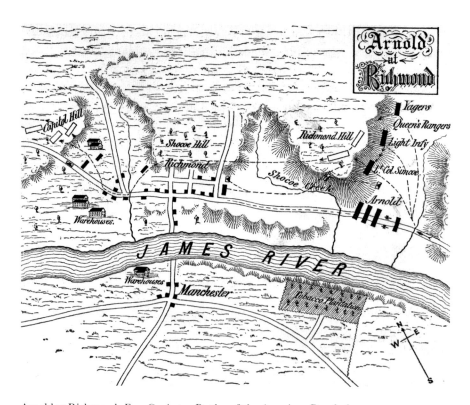

Arnold at Richmond. *From Carrington,* Battles of the American Revolution.

cartridge boxes, bayonets, musket cartridges and a magazine mill. Two to three hundred Virginia militia troops led by Major Alexander Dick fired a volley at Simcoe's Queen's Rangers in the vanguard of Arnold's column prior to falling back prudently from their position on Church Hill, but the British encountered no other opposition.[32]

The raiders left Richmond around noon on January 6, marched southeast and camped at Four Mile Creek along the New Market Road, north of Deep Bottom. Arnold then proceeded to Berkeley Plantation on the James River, freed some of the slaves there and, on January 10, boarded his ships to sail downstream. A landing party of five hundred redcoats met some opposition from militia at Hood's Point (near the mouth of Wards Creek, in Prince George County), but the Virginians were driven off by a determined British bayonet charge. After looting Smithfield and Cobham on the south side of the river, Arnold disembarked his soldiers at Portsmouth on January 19 in order to establish a base there in accordance with Clinton's orders. Although almost four thousand militiamen gathered to defend the Tidewater area against Arnold's excursion, they were divided between Fredericksburg, Williamsburg and Cabin Point, on the south side of the James. Virginia's response was slow and hesitant, for which Jefferson received much of the blame.[33] "The greatest distress we now feel," wrote Continental major general Baron von Steuben, then serving in the beleaguered commonwealth, "is the want of arms," and the men lacked basic camp equipment as well. The troops were "in want of everything; and nothing can be got from the state, rather for want of arrangement than anything else."[34]

Clinton ordered more troops from the New York garrison to the Chesapeake in March. On the twenty-seventh, General Phillips arrived at Portsmouth with two thousand men, including two battalions of light infantry, the Forty-third Regiment of Foot, Seventy-sixth (Highland) Regiment, part of the Seventeenth Regiment of Foot, the Hessian Fusilier Regiment Erbprinz, Hessian artillery and the First and Second Anspach-Bayreuth regiments.[35] His orders from Clinton were to destroy rebel supply caches along the James and Appomattox Rivers, cooperate with Cornwallis and "interrupt the course of supplies to the Carolinas." Upon landing his men in Virginia, Phillips soon strengthened the defenses of Portsmouth, which he judged unsuitable upon his inspection.[36]

Meanwhile, British vessels were active on the state's tidal rivers, raiding plantations and plundering property—even Mount Vernon, Washington's home eight miles south of Alexandria. A squadron of privateers and the British navy sloop HMS *Savage*, commanded by Captain Richard Graves, had been operating on the upper Potomac for over a week, in part to prevent any rebel troops from crossing the river at Alexandria and marching south. Capturing prizes was also part of their mission. A British ship tried to seize commercial vessels from the town's docks in early April but was chased off and captured downriver. On April 12, an enemy party from the *Savage* landed at Mount Vernon, which was under the management of Washington's cousin, Lund Washington. Lund provided supplies for the enemy's ships after British officers demanded provisions or they would burn the general's house. Eighteen Mount Vernon slaves escaped to the flotilla, which departed the area soon thereafter.[37]

Lafayette later reported this incident to the commanding general, stating that it would "certainly Have a Bad effect, and Contrasts with Spirited Answers from Some Neighbours that Had their Houses Burnt Accordingly... You will do what you think proper about it, my dear general; but, as your friend, it was my duty confidentially to mention the circumstances."[38] Upon receipt of a letter from his cousin describing the British visit to the estate, General Washington was unhappy at the report. "No man can condemn the measure more than I do," he later told Lafayette, regretting that Lund acted as "more the trustee and guardian of my property than the representative of my honor."[39] To his cousin, he wrote with some anger that "it would have been a less painful circumstance to me, to have heard, that in consequence

George Washington's home, Mount Vernon, was raided by British forces in April 1781. *Library of Congress.*

of your non-compliance with their request, they had burnt my House, and laid the Plantation in ruins."[40]

By early June, the enemy's privateers were so active in the rivers filling the Chesapeake Bay that even British general Leslie complained about them. He told Cornwallis that these "rascally privateers" ravaged riverside plantations and seemed not to differentiate friend from foe. "Some stop must be put to it," he wrote, "for our friends complain bitterly of it."[41]

While British ships looted Virginia planters, the main enemy effort was Phillips's operations in the Tidewater. Three weeks after disembarking, Phillips took 2,500 soldiers and moved up the James River in eleven ships on April 18, leaving behind a small garrison at Portsmouth. Landing the next day at Burwell's Ferry on the north bank of the James, the troops marched west and quickly captured nearby Williamsburg and Yorktown, brushing aside General Nelson's "500 militia...who retired upon our approach," as most lacked muskets. The light infantry burned Virginia's shipyard, "several armed ships" and warehouses situated on the Chickahominy River on the twentieth, along with other supplies at Diascund Bridge in New Kent County.[42] Continuing westward, on April 23, his troops made camp on the banks of the James River at Westover.[43]

Westover, the Byrd family home where Cornwallis's army encamped after crossing the James River. *Library of Congress.*

Governor Jefferson knew of the arrival of the new expedition in Chesapeake Bay by March 21 but was unsure of its strength or objective. "Should this army from Portsmouth come forth and become active," Jefferson wrote to Virginia's congressmen in Philadelphia, "our affairs will assume a very disagreeable aspect." He lamented that the state had sent militiamen to reinforce Greene in the Carolinas and maintained thousands of troops in the Ohio Valley to guard against Indian depredations, leaving the commonwealth ill-prepared to meet the present danger at home. From all over eastern Virginia, demands came in from militia officers begging for arms, ammunition and other supplies—none of which Jefferson or the state's commissaries could deliver.[44] Baron von Steuben, suspecting that the British intended to strike Petersburg upon seeing their numerous transport and warships in the river off Westover, ordered General Muhlenberg to bring his men closer to the town and the valuable supplies stored there. Muhlenberg first went to Prince George Court House, east of Petersburg, to block the enemy's anticipated line of march and to remove all military stores collected there. His militia units then moved back to Blandford on April 24 on orders from von Steuben.[45]

The baron had guessed correctly: Phillips's objective was indeed Petersburg, where he intended to destroy rebel supplies and more easily act in concert with Cornwallis in North Carolina.[46] Soon, the British army landed at City Point, at the confluence of the Appomattox and James Rivers, and began an overland march to take Petersburg, some ten miles distant. Upon receiving word of the British landing, the town was in a panic, as local authorities scrambled to haul off any remaining stores. Von Steuben decided to transfer his men to the north side of the Appomattox River on high ground overlooking the city while Colonel Dick's troops were posted at Blandford as a rear guard. Once the enemy approached, however, von Steuben elected to risk a battle even though his all-militia force of one thousand men was outnumbered. As the general later wrote, "Without some show of resistance" the British "would have intimidated the inhabitants and encouraged the enemy to further incursions."[47]

Phillips advanced along the River Road, on the south side of the Appomattox River. Von Steuben moved his men back into Petersburg, where he placed his first line of five hundred men in an advantageous position east of Blandford on the west bank of Poor Creek. His second defensive line was posted on the east side of Petersburg overlooking Lieutenant Run as far north as the river, and part of his force was held in reserve to the rear. Although the Virginians were posted on high ground with

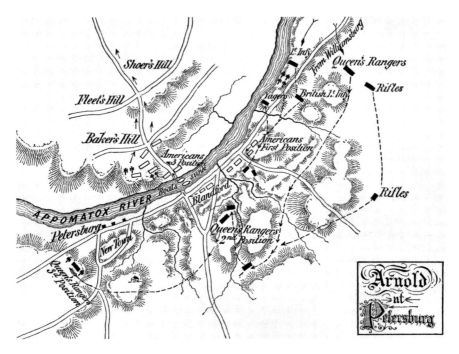

Arnold at Petersburg. *From Carrington,* Battles of the American Revolution.

creeks in their front, these militiamen faced battle-hardened redcoats under experienced officers determined to take the town.[48]

In the afternoon, Phillips deployed his force in battle lines. He ordered part of his troops to attack the American right flank and turn it while the rest of his men moved forward against von Steuben's front. Phillips also directed Simcoe to make a sweeping movement around the American right with his cavalry, the light infantry and Hessian jaegers, nimble troops armed with highly accurate rifles. While Simcoe moved undetected to the south around the Patriot militia lines, a waterborne attack of eleven flatboats from the Appomattox River by more of Phillips's troops startled the Americans, but a small force of militia volunteers managed to repulse it before being driven off themselves by enemy fire.[49]

When the British brought up their artillery to high ground and fired on the Virginians in the first line, von Steuben ordered these men to withdraw to the town. As the redcoats advanced, Patriot artillery fired on them from across the river on Baker's Hill. The militia steadfastly repulsed several determined frontal attacks from Phillips's infantry regiments, attacking the second line in the course of an hour. Jefferson heard reports that the attacking redcoats "broke twice & run like Sheep till supported by fresh Troops." When the Royal Artillery guns were brought up again to pound the American lines, however, von Steuben and Muhlenberg recognized the time had come to retreat across the river. "The superior number of the enemy and a want of ammunition obliged me to order a retreat & the [Appomattox] bridge to be taken up which was executed in the greatest order notwithstanding the fire of the enemy cannon and musketry," the baron proudly reported to General Greene. The militia retreated northward, although at times, the British managed to get close enough that the combat was hand to hand. Simcoe soon brought up his wing of the assault and pressed von Steuben's rear. The Patriot units crossed the bridge while losing some prisoners to the enemy, but when they began to climb the hill on the north bank of the river, British artillery turned the retreat into disorder. The Americans lost 150 men in the three-hour battle but were able to regroup once out of cannon range. They marched north to Chesterfield Court House, although many militiamen fell out of the ranks and went home. "I cannot but congratulate you on the initiation of our militia into the business of war," Jefferson wrote to von Steuben, "general actions I dare say you will think should not be risked but with great advantages, but the more the militia are employed in the small way, the more contentedly they will remain, and they will improve the more."[50]

Petersburg was now in the hands of the invaders. After the battle, Phillips's troops burned tobacco in the town and destroyed several ships on the Appomattox River. They also repaired the bridge over the river, marched north and encamped briefly at Ampthill, a plantation belonging to prominent Patriot Archibald Cary, located about four miles south of Richmond.[51] On April 27, the redcoats moved to Osborne's Landing, a plantation wharf and tobacco inspection point a dozen miles below Richmond on the south bank of the James in a neck of land called Bermuda Hundred.[52]

On the twenty-seventh, Phillips led the light infantry, part of the Queen's Rangers cavalry and some Hessian jaegers north; dispersed some militia companies at Chesterfield Court House; and burned a large barracks there along with other public buildings. Most of von Steuben's men had prudently left the small village upon the enemy's approach. Simultaneously, Arnold took three regiments and a detachment of the Queen's Rangers to Osborne's Landing, where after skirmishing with the Virginia militia, his troops captured a dozen ships "loaded with tobacco, cordage, flour, etc." and burned several vessels of the Virginia navy before Phillips's soldiers joined him. All the troops remained at Osborne's Landing the following day before moving upstream.[53]

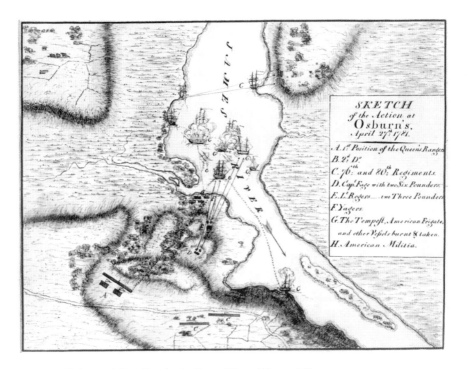

SKETCH
of the Action at
Osburn's.
April 27th 1781.

A. 1st Position of the Queens Rangers
B. 2d Do.
C. 76th and 80th Regiments.
D. Capt Fage with two Six Pounders.
E. Lt Rogers ... two Three Pounders
F. Yagers
G. The Tempest, American Frigate,
and other Vessels burnt & taken.
H. American Militia.

Action at Osbourne's Landing, in the James River. *Library of Congress.*

On April 29, Phillips's column reached Manchester, opposite Richmond, and burned wheat, flour, corn, tobacco warehouses, supplies, boats and equipment. Here, however, Phillips received word that in Richmond over one thousand Continental light troops had just arrived under the command of Lafayette and were supported by a militia contingent of unknown strength. In fact, Lafayette's force occupied Shockoe Hill in a strong position above Phillips's likely river crossing point at Rockett's Landing, which made the British commander pause in his original plan to sack Virginia's new capital. Phillips's attempt to put part of his troops across the James was turned back by a bold counterstroke by mounted Patriot troops. With some exaggeration, Jefferson reported this repulse to Washington two weeks later: "Six or eight hundred of their picked men of the light Infantry with General Arnold at their Head having crossed the River from Warwick fled from a Patrole of 16 Horse every man into his boat as he could some pushing North & some South as their Fears drove them."[54]

After considering his options for a few days, Phillips led his army south from Warwick to Osborne's Landing and embarked in ships at Bermuda Hundred on May 2 for a return to Portsmouth. While on the river, however,

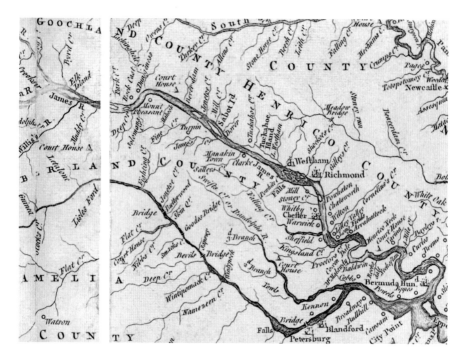

Region between Richmond and Petersburg. *North Carolina Collection, University of North Carolina–Chapel Hill.*

he received firm intelligence on May 7 that Cornwallis and his veterans were marching to Petersburg from North Carolina. With this news, Phillips and his troops returned "with a fair wind" back to Petersburg by May 9, having landed most of the troops two days earlier at Brandon, an old plantation of the Harrison family in Prince George County.[55]

When the redcoats reached Petersburg, Phillips's health had declined such that he retired to Bollingbrook, the home of Mary Marshall Tabb Bolling, on East Hill above the falls of the Appomattox River. The general was "reduced" by a debilitating fever that prevented him from writing to Clinton himself. He was, wrote Arnold on May 12, "incapable of business, and the physicians are not without fears for his safety." The doctors were correct in their worries, as Phillips died the next day. One week later, Cornwallis's exhausted column marched into Petersburg from the south.[56]

3

"A DIFFICULT AND DANGEROUS EXPEDITION"

Lafayette Comes to Defend Virginia

O now, who will behold
The royal captain of this ruin'd tent,
Walking from watch to watch, from tent to tent,
Let him cry, "Praise and Glory on his head!"
For forth he goes, and visits all his host,
Bids them good morrow with a modest smile,
And calls them brothers, friends, and countrymen.
—Shakespeare, Henry V, *Act 4, Prologue*

Since June 1775, General George Washington had nominally been in command of all Continental forces. He was, however, unable to exert direct control of military affairs in the Southern Department during the Revolutionary War until late in the conflict due to distance, prevailing communication difficulties of the eighteenth century and his own unrelenting burdens of command in the northern colonies. Although he did offer guidance to southern theater commanders; sent what limited supplies and reinforcements he could to armies battling the British and Loyalists in Virginia, the Carolinas and Georgia; and advised Congress on military appointments, Washington's role in operations and campaigns in the South was limited until the 1781 Siege of Yorktown, Virginia. Nevertheless, he assigned three of his best major generals to the Southern Department beginning in October 1780, which he hoped would ensure American success in the distant

Major General Nathanael Greene, the American commander of the Southern Department. *Library of Congress.*

theater. Two of the officers, the Marquis de Lafayette and Nathanael Greene, exceeded his expectations, but Baron von Steuben met little success in his efforts to assist Virginia's war effort.[57]

The twin South Carolina disasters in 1780—the surrender of Charles Town in May and the humiliating defeat of General Gates's Continental Army at Camden in August—forced Washington and Congress to pay closer attention to the situation in the Southern Department. The British had been concentrating more of their forces in the South since December 1778, and even after the Whig victory at Kings Mountain in October 1780, the enemy's operations in the Carolinas seemed likely to conquer both states and now threatened Virginia. Accordingly, Washington offered what limited assistance he could.

To replace Horatio Gates as commander of the Southern Department, Washington chose Major General Nathanael Greene, a Rhode Island officer who had served in the Continental Army since 1775. After early setbacks in New York and New Jersey as an inexperienced commander, by the time he received his new assignment in October 1780, Greene was the obvious choice to command in the South and had earned his commander's confidence. Greene's efficient—though unheralded—service as Washington's quartermaster general from March 1778 to August 1780 would prove useful in the Carolinas, where he struggled to arm, feed, clothe and equip his ragged troops until the end of the war. Although Greene did not lead operations in Virginia or participate in the Siege of Yorktown, he was in continual contact with Lafayette, Thomas Jefferson, Thomas Nelson Jr., Baron von Steuben and other authorities in Virginia regarding supplies, recruiting and provisions during his ultimately successful tenure in the South. He assumed departmental command at Charlotte, North Carolina, on December 3, 1780.[58]

On Greene's long journey from Washington's army in New York to his new headquarters at Charlotte, he was accompanied by Baron von Steuben, who was assigned to help Greene reestablish a viable Patriot force in the Southern Department after the disastrous summer there. Recognizing that Virginia would provide him with most of the soldiers and materiel he would need in the war-torn Carolinas, Greene left von Steuben in the Old Dominion to oversee the logistical system needed to support American forces in the South and to recruit, drill and organize Continental soldiers for active operations. Von Steuben was a talented organizer and drillmaster and was the primary architect of the more professional Continental Army that emerged from the miserable winter camps at Valley Forge, Pennsylvania, in 1778. After this valuable service to Washington, the commander in chief appointed him inspector general, a new position in which the Prussian acted in the role of Washington's chief of staff.[59] Von Steuben would prove to be a tireless officer in his efforts to support Greene and in helping Virginia defend itself against the British invasions of 1780 and 1781. Eventually, however, his relationship with Governor Jefferson and other state officials became contentious, and he achieved little success in the field.[60]

After receiving disheartening reports of the destructive raids by Leslie and Arnold, Washington decided to send regular troops from New York to Virginia since the state's militia force was incapable of halting the British depredations. Washington—and many other American officers—had a long-held aversion to the use of militia instead of professional troops, going back to his French and Indian War campaigning in the 1750s. His Continental Army service had done nothing to disabuse him of these opinions. "We shall never be able to resist [the enemy's] force," he advised Congress in 1777, "if the Militia are to be relied on."[61] Reports of Gates's 1780 defeat at Camden prompted the commander in chief to reflect that he "never was witness to a single instance that can countenance an opinion of Militia or raw troops being fit for the real business of fighting."[62] Perhaps his most succinct observation of the militia's questionable value during the Revolutionary War was that "to place any dependence on Militia, is assuredly, resting upon a broken reed."[63]

German illustration of an American rifleman and a light infantryman. *Library of Congress.*

In mid-February, Washington fixed on a plan to send to the South a force of about 1,200 light infantrymen, special troops trained, armed and equipped to allow for quick movement, skirmishing and for reconnaissance. Washington initially organized "a corps of light infantry" in 1777, with troops expected to "be constantly near the enemy and [to] give 'em every possible annoyance." By the following year, all light units were only to enroll "the best men, the most hardy and active marksmen, commanded by good partizan officers."[64] In 1778, the Continental Army was reorganized, including the formation of light infantry troops numbering up to 2,600 men by the following year. These new companies scored a notable success in July 1779 at the Battle of Stony Point, New York, in which a British garrison on the Hudson River was overwhelmed by light troops in a nighttime bayonet assault. Later, two brigades of light infantry were formed into a division and commanded by Lafayette in 1780. For southern service in 1781, Washington ordered the light companies in the army to be "completed to fifty rank and file each" and to assemble at Peekskill, New York. This Continental detachment consisted of three battalions of Massachusetts, Connecticut, Rhode Island, New Hampshire and New Jersey light companies and one light company from Hazen's Second Canadian Regiment, augmented by three regular infantry companies of the New Jersey line.[65] It was necessary, Washington ordered, to have "the men robust and in other respects well chosen" and ready to march by February 19 at the latest.[66] Washington hoped that the forces sent to Virginia would help capture the traitor Arnold at his Portsmouth base, which would be "an event particularly agreeable to this Country."[67]

Washington's plan to reinforce Virginia with his own troops in New York was a derivative of his long-sought goal to coordinate operations with the allied French navy in American waters. During the early winter of 1780–81, the British maintained a fleet under Vice-Admiral Arbuthnot in the protective waters of Gardiner's Bay, off eastern Long Island. From this anchorage British ships kept a French fleet bottled up in Newport, Rhode Island. The French, however, became more aggressive once Rear Admiral Chevalier Destouches took over command at Newport in December 1780. After learning that a storm had crippled three of Arbuthnot's ships of the line in late January, Destouches decided to send a sixty-four-gun warship and two frigates to the mouth of the Chesapeake Bay in February, in order to carry desperately needed muskets to Virginia. More importantly, Destouches hoped to prevent Arnold from receiving supplies at Portsmouth by blocking the entrance to the bay and to destroy the turncoat's transport ships at anchor. The French admiral sent his three ships from Newport on February 9 under Captain Arnaud le Gardeur de Tilly, although neither the arms for Virginia nor the troops were shipped with this expedition.[68]

Washington hoped that sending his Continental light companies to the Virginia Tidewater to coordinate with the French in an attack on Portsmouth would "give the enterprise all possible chance of success." The American general beseeched the Comte de Rochambeau, lieutenant general and commander of a powerful French expeditionary force sent to America in the summer of 1780, to send a force to the Chesapeake to relieve the embattled southern states. The February operation, however, was not well coordinated. Destouches seems not to have considered how he would get his large ships up the Elizabeth River to attack Portsmouth, and he departed Newport before Washington had any hopes of getting troops to the lower Chesapeake Bay in time to cooperate with the French naval force.[69]

Meanwhile, Washington proceeded with his preparations to snare Arnold. To lead the light infantry detachment to Virginia, he chose Lafayette.[70] In his written instructions to the young Frenchman, Washington informed him that his troops were to move quickly overland to the "top" of the Chesapeake Bay at Head of Elk, Maryland. "Leave good officers to bring up the tired, lazy, and drunken Soldiers" on the march to Maryland, Washington advised the young general several days later. Lafayette was to bring his men by water from Head of Elk to Hampton, Virginia, to coordinate with Destouches' ships, which would presumably be in nearby waters. "When you arrive at your destination," Washington stated, "you must act as your own judgment and the circumstances shall direct."[71]

Major General the Marquis de Lafayette. *Library of Congress.*

The commanding general also advised his protégé to coordinate with von Steuben before his arrival at Hampton, so that the latter might "have a sufficient body of militia ready to act in conjunction with your detachment." If Benedict Arnold were captured during the course of the operations, "you will execute [him] in the most summary way," Washington ordered.[72] The marquis acted promptly upon receiving this assignment and left the army's New York headquarters along the Hudson River by February 22.[73]

Lafayette's detachment would also receive reinforcements. In order to bolster American forces in the South, on February 20, Congress ordered that most of the Pennsylvania regiments in Continental service would thenceforth "compose part of the Southern Army" and must move to Virginia as soon as they were ready, in small detachments if necessary. Washington also ordered that the first brigade of these troops should be sent to Virginia under the command Brigadier General Anthony Wayne, an aggressive young officer with extensive combat experience.[74]

Washington's choice to lead the light infantry detachment to Virginia was one of the most colorful figures in American military history. Gilbert du Motier, the Marquis de Lafayette, was born into a noble French family of great wealth in 1757. His father, a French army officer, was killed in 1759 by a cannonball at the Battle of Minden in Westphalia during the Seven Years' War, an engagement in which British general Phillips also participated as a young artillery officer—a fact well known to the marquis. Lafayette chose a military career as well, serving as a captain in the Musketeers of the Guard. Resentment of the British and an exuberant interest in the American struggle for liberty led the marquis to embrace their enlightened cause and travel to the rebellious colonies in 1777. Against the orders of King Louis

XVI, Lafayette left France and crossed the Atlantic Ocean, landing in South Carolina. He had been assured of a Continental Army commission by an American agent in France, so after a brief visit to Charles Town, the marquis and his entourage rode hundreds of miles north to present themselves to Congress in Philadelphia in late July.

By the time he arrived there, however, Congress had largely soured on commissioning foreign officers, but it accepted Lafayette's gracious offer to serve without pay as a major general. Joining Washington's headquarters staff, the American commander in chief took a liking to the enthusiastic nineteen-year-old nobleman who was still learning to speak English, although most historians (and Lafayette) later romanticized and exaggerated the nature of this so-called father-and-son relationship. While the gregarious Frenchman quickly came to regard Washington as a father figure, it is clear from Washington's correspondence that the elder Virginian saw Lafayette as an intimate friend rather than a son. Nevertheless, the two men became quite

Generals Washington and Lafayette in winter camp at Valley Forge, Pennsylvania. *Library of Congress.*

close. While serving with Washington's army, Lafayette experienced combat at the Battle of Brandywine in 1777 (where he was wounded in his left leg), the Battles of Monmouth Courthouse and Rhode Island in 1778 and several smaller engagements, earning Washington's respect for his bravery, abilities and capacity for independent command.[75]

A week after Lafayette left the army's New York encampment, Washington wrote to him with revised instructions. The Continental commander apprised him that in North Carolina, Greene's exhausted army was retreating before Lord Cornwallis and that he (Washington) was also concerned that Arnold and his troops might escape before Destouches' fleet could trap him at Portsmouth. This intelligence induced Washington to give the marquis "greater latitude than you had in your original instructions." He was now empowered to "concert a plan with the French General and Naval Commander for a descent into North Carolina; to cut off the detachment of the enemy, which had ascended Cape Fear River, intercept if possible Cornwallis, and relieve General Greene and the Southern states." Washington went on to declare that this was a "secondary object" and that there "should be strong reasons to induce a change of our first plan against Arnold, if he is still in Virginia." Washington had earlier advised the marquis not to move his soldiers beyond Head of Elk without first coordinating support from the French fleet at the Virginia Capes. Nevertheless, Lafayette was given extraordinary discretion in governing his own course of action.[76]

Slogging over muddy roads, Lafayette's column had reached Philadelphia by March 2. The men marched with "order and Alacrity," he reported, perhaps because Congress had just given the soldiers one month's advance pay. To help prepare for active operations upon his arrival in Virginia, the marquis sent a staff officer ahead to alert von Steuben of his progress. "Nothing on our part Has Been wanting for the Success of the Expedition," he reported in one of many letters to Washington.[77]

Still, both Lafayette and Washington were disappointed in early March with news that the three ships sent by Destouches to Chesapeake waters were unable to ascend the Elizabeth River to attack Arnold's garrison or the enemy's vessels at Portsmouth. "They could do nothing more than block up the river," Jefferson lamented. De Tilly remained at the entrance to the bay for several days catching smaller enemy ships with false colors, but by February 24, the French expedition was back at Newport—just two days after Lafayette left New York. Without French naval support, Lafayette complained that now his "Expectations are not Great, and I think we Have But few chances for us. I Shall make all possible dispatch, and listen

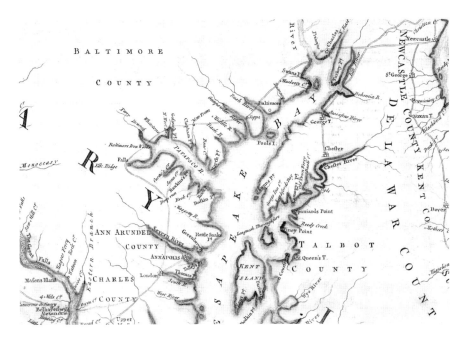

The upper Chesapeake Bay. *North Carolina Collection, University of North Carolina-Chapel Hill.*

particularly to the Voice of prudence. However some Hazard must Be Ran, if we Undertake in this Circumstances."[78]

Lafayette was soon thereafter encouraged to learn that after de Tilly had sailed back to Newport, Destouches decided to bring his entire fleet to Virginia waters, along with about 1,200 infantrymen. Rochambeau wrote to Washington on February 25 that "the great importance which it has seemed to me that your Excellency attaches to the gaining of a foothold by Arnold has determined M. Destouches to sacrifice everything with that in view."[79]

After reaching Head of Elk, Lafayette learned that the boats needed to transport his men down the Chesapeake Bay had yet to arrive. "Contrary Winds, Heavy Rains, Disappointments of vessels And Every Inconvenience to which we Had No Remedy Have Been from the day of My Arrival Combined Against our Embarkation," he reported in frustration to Washington on March 7.[80] On the following day, he advised his commander that a "Great deal Must Be personally Risked—But I Hope to Manage things so as to Commit no imprudence with the excellent detachment whose glory is as dear and whose Safety is much dearer to me than My own."[81]

By March 9, Lafayette had arranged shipping for his troops to sail to Annapolis while he preceded them to Maryland's capital, intending to go on to the lower Chesapeake to coordinate with the French squadron he expected there. Leaving the soldiers at Annapolis, he pressed on and reached Yorktown, Virginia, on the fourteenth, and there wrote to General Wayne to encourage him to bring his Pennsylvania troops to Virginia for an attack on Portsmouth. The marquis continued on to Suffolk and then, with General Muhlenberg, reconnoitered Arnold's defensive works at Portsmouth, outside of which were deployed about 1,500 Virginia militia troops. After appraising the strong enemy defenses there, Lafayette retired to Williamsburg by March 23.[82]

The marquis was disappointed to hear of no French ships off the Virginia Capes since Washington had recently advised him that Rochambeau planned to send his entire fleet (including eight ships of the line) under Destouches to Chesapeake Bay to help bag Arnold's garrison. Once again, American hopes for French naval support were dashed. On March 16, off Cape Henry, Virginia, the French encountered ships of Arbuthnot's British fleet, which had chased them from Long Island and fought a tactically inconclusive sea battle. However, after the fighting, Arbuthnot took a position with his ships just inside Chesapeake Bay, thwarting the French attempt to trap Arnold. "The French squadron gained a great deal of glory, whilst the English attained their desired end," Lafayette wrote to his wife in August, betraying his frustration with the French naval commanders in America. Destouches set sail for Newport the following day.[83]

It was the news of the French fleet returning to Rhode Island after the sea battle on the sixteenth that prompted General Clinton in New York to send to Virginia under General Phillips British reinforcements, which began to arrive at Lynnhaven Bay by March 25. Aware now of this new British expedition to the Chesapeake, Lafayette decided to return to Annapolis, where his troops remained bivouacked, in case new orders had arrived there from Washington. Arriving at the small port city on April 4, he wrote to Greene that since the French ships had returned northward, he had "nothing to do but to return to the Grand Army" under Washington, per his previous instructions. "As soon as the enterprise has either succeeded or miscarried," Washington had earlier stipulated, Lafayette was "to return immediately" to New York. The marquis brought his men north to Head of Elk a few days later, having driven off two small British ships lurking in the waters by Maryland's capital. The commanding general did, in fact, direct the marquis to bring his light infantry battalions from Maryland back to New York by a letter dated April 5, but the next day, he reconsidered these orders and instead directed Lafayette to "join the southern Army" under General Greene "as expeditiously as possible." Having consulted with his senior officers, Washington altered Lafayette's mission after considering "of what vast importance it will be to reinforce Genl Greene as speedily as possible, more especially as there can be little doubt but the detachment under Genl Phillips, if not part of that now under the command of Genl Arnold, will ultimately join, or, in some degree, cooperate with Lord Cornwallis." With Arnold and Phillips both in Virginia, Washington concluded, Lafayette and his small force were needed even more in the South.[84]

In North Carolina, Greene heard rumors from von Steuben that Lafayette planned to return to New York. "I cannot think this can be advisable," he wrote to the marquis on April 3. With the British concentrating their efforts in the South, Greene advised that "the very critical situation of the Southern States and the fatal consequences that must attend your drawing off your force if the enemy push their operations as they most undoubtedly will induces me to wish you to March your force Southward by Alexandria & Fredericksburg to Richmond." There, Lafayette could either support Greene or the militia in the Virginia Tidewater "as the movements of the Enemy may render necessary." Greene concluded his letter with flattery. "It would afford me great pleasure to have you with the Southern Army," he wrote, "and here is a sufficient field to exercise your genius and gratify your ambition."[85]

Receiving Washington's new orders at Head of Elk, Lafayette made preparations to return to Virginia. Since many of his soldiers were from regiments of northern states, however, a number of them grew "uneasy at the idea of joining the Southern Army." Most of them were destitute,[86] and his battalions were lacking "tents, overalls, shirts, shoes" and ammunition. Although Washington sent 1,200 shirts, linen overalls, pairs of shoes and socks to Lafayette from New York in April, they would no doubt take weeks to arrive at the light troops' southern camps. To General Greene, the marquis penned a dreadful description of his small corps as they marched to the south. His officers had

> *No money, no baggage of any sort, no summer clothes, and hardly a shirt to shift. To these common miseries the soldiers added their shocking naked*[ness and a] *want of shoes etc. etc. Having been thus conducted to Trenton, they were hurried on board vessels and having been embarked at* [Head of] *Elk they arrived at Annapolis where the hope of a short expedition against Arnold silenced every complaint and kept of their spirits. They had hitherto been in houses or on board of vessels, so that it was impossible they would feel the extreme want of tents which however crowded with officers and men*

leave a number of them to sleep in open air. Camp kettles could be borrowed
in towns or from vessels, and blankets were almost unnecessary.

With the expectation that they would soon return northward, the men were "recomforted" at the "pleasant prospect of returning towards home, seeing their wives...And getting large sums of money," the troops grew unruly when ordered back to Virginia. "The officers did not like it More than the men, and the men...began to desert in great numbers."[87] To Washington, he reported from the Susquehanna River that his men would rather suffer a "hundred lashes than journey to the Southward." Some of his troops deserted on account of their dread of campaigning in the South during the upcoming hot and humid summer months. "The New England troops have taken an idea that southern climates are very unwholesome and that of Carolina mortal to them," the marquis reported to Greene.[88]

Once across the Susquehanna at Harmer's Town (now Havre de Grace), Maryland, the wide river acted as a barrier for further desertions, as did the prompt execution of a recaptured deserter. The column had marched through Baltimore by April 18, where the troops were in better spirits after the marquis' personal exertions. "I Made an order for the troops wherein I Endeavoured to throw a kind of Infamy upon desertion, and to improve every particular affection of theirs—Since that, desertion Has Been lessened," he reported. In his memoirs, Lafayette described (in the third person) his predicament:

> *Lafayette issued an order, declaring that he was setting out for a difficult and dangerous expedition; that he hoped that the soldiers would not abandon him, but that whoever wished to go away might do so instantly; and he sent away two soldiers who had just been punished for some serious offences. From that hour all desertions ceased, and not one man would leave him: this feeling was so strong, that an under officer, who was prevented by a diseased leg from following the detachment, hired, at his own expense, a cart, rather than separate from it.*

As the men were "shockingly destitute of linen," Lafayette used £2,000 of his personal credit to secure much-needed supplies and clothing for the troops, which Washington assured him would "entitle you to all their gratitude & affection, and will, at the same time that it endears your Name (if possible still more) to this Country; be an everlasting monument of your ardent zeal & attachment to its cause & the establishment of its Independence."[89]

With news of British raids along the James River in April, Lafayette stripped his column of heavy baggage, wagons and artillery, which were to follow the soldiers from Baltimore. "This Rapid mode of travelling added to My other precautions will I Hope keep up our Spirits and Satisfaction," he reported. Crossing the Potomac River in flatboats after a two-day overland march, the troops reached, on April 21, the small port town of Alexandria, Virginia, where the Frenchman noted that the "Men are in High Spirits."[90]

Morale might have been high, but the troops sent south to provide succor for Virginia were still in pitiable condition. "In our Absolute Want of Shoes and Cloathes of Every Kind," Lafayette wrote to Governor Jefferson, "it is impossible for the Men to Make such Rapid Marches Unless we Have An extraordinary Help of Horses and Waggons." He told the governor that his men were so "Entirely destitute of Shoes that Unless a large Number of them is Collected the feet of our Men will Be So sore As to Make it impossible for them to Advance." Lafayette was unable to secure any wagons at Alexandria without using impressment, an unavoidable but burdensome means of official confiscation never popular with the citizenry.[91]

Although his troops were exhausted upon entering Virginia, the marquis had overcome many logistical difficulties and arrived with his soldiers for active service in the Southern Department. Far to the south, Cornwallis was still in Wilmington, contemplating a march northward to vanquish Virginia. Closer to Lafayette, but still days away, Phillips was proceeding up the James River, intent on capturing Petersburg. Though unaware of his enemy's plans, Lafayette knew time was of the essence once he arrived at Alexandria. After resting his men briefly, the marquis ordered their march to resume southward on the dusty King's Highway toward Richmond.

On April 25, the marquis' corps of light infantry reached Fredericksburg on the Rappahannock River, after a tiring march in "extreme heat." No wagons were immediately available to transport most of his provisions or ammunition because the inhabitants hid them—and their horses—as the Continental soldiers approached. "As soon As we get this Necessary Article," he advised Jefferson, the troops "will Rapidly proceed to Richmond, And Notwithstanding the fatigues of the March will on their Arrival Be Ready for Serious Operations." Lafayette was not surprised by "the difficulties We Meet with in the Road" and resignedly concluded that "When we Are not able to do what we Wish, we Must do what we Can." He planned to ride ahead of his troops and the baggage train by way of Bowling Green and Hanover Court House on his way to Richmond, the state's new capital. For his safety he asked Jefferson to send some dragoons to Hanover for an

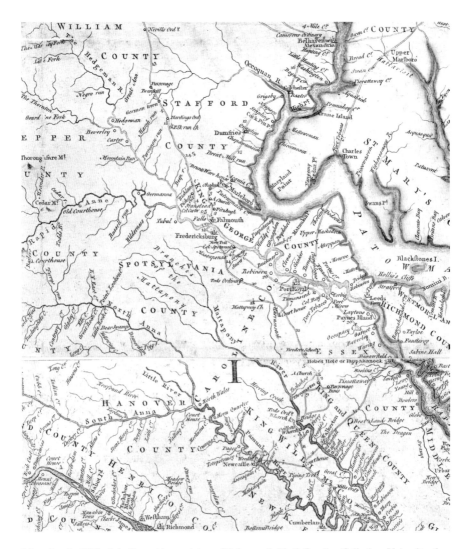

Map detail of Virginia from Alexandria to Richmond. *North Carolina Collection, University of North Carolina–Chapel Hill.*

escort. "Upon Your Excellency is all our dependance [*sic*] for provisions," he flattered the governor.[92]

After passing through Hanover Court House ahead of his troops on April 28, Lafayette met Governor Jefferson at Richmond later that day or the next. Once the Continentals arrived at Richmond on the afternoon of the twenty-ninth, they were posted on the east end of the town at Rocketts Landing.[93] It was here that they arrived just in time to thwart Phillips's attempt to enter Richmond from the opposite side of the James River. Soon thereafter, Lafayette received word from Greene in South Carolina directing him to take command in Virginia "and conduct the military operations as circumstances shall dictate to be proper." Greene also warned Lafayette "not to let the love of fame get the better of your prudence and plunge you into a misfortune, in too eager a pursuit after glory." Greene doubtlessly felt compelled to offer this cautionary advice to the young French noble due to the latter's well-known desire to win military fame in the America war. Lafayette's summer campaign in Virginia would soon demonstrate that he took this counsel to heart.[94]

The marquis' arrival at the Virginia capital with his soldiers was certainly timely. "Our forced march saved Richmond," Lafayette reported several weeks later. He initially expected Phillips to join Cornwallis in North Carolina, and he "was determined to follow him, and should have Risked every thing Rather than to omit making a diversion in favor of Greene." However, when the British moved to Petersburg, Lafayette was instead "obliged…to stick to this [north] Side of the [James] River from whence Reinforcements are expected." The Frenchman had with him about nine hundred to one thousand Continentals, who found "the climate very warm but do not desert." He noted with alarm that the redcoats were much stronger, especially in cavalry, and he still had not heard from General Wayne, whom he assumed was marching south from Pennsylvania. "The enemy are more than double our force in regular troops," he reported to Greene, "and their command of the water gives them great advantages." Moreover, the Virginia militia at Richmond "are not numerous, come without arms, and are not used to war." The state government "wants energy, and there is nothing to enforce the laws," while the various departments and bureaus were "in the greatest Confusion and Relaxation. Nothing can Be obtained and yet expenses were enormous." Acknowledging his inability to stand up to the British forces, he sought to "improve so as to receive one Blow that, Being Beat, I may at least Be Beat with some decency." Once Wayne's troops arrived he hoped that "Cornwallis shall pay some thing for his victory," but he lamented that "the Command of the waters, the Superiority in Cavalry, and the great disproportion of forces, gave the Ennemy such advantages that I durst not venture out and listen to my fondness for enterprise. To speak truth I was afraid of myself as much as of the Enemy. Independence has rendered me the more cautious, as I know my own warmth."[95]

Aware of Cornwallis's approach from North Carolina, Lafayette crossed the James River at Richmond on May 7, intent on a thrust to Petersburg, but British forces beat him to it and even captured some of his staff officers who had ridden ahead of the main body of Continentals. After bombarding British forces in Petersburg with four guns from the north side of the Appomattox on May 10, Lafayette returned his troops to Richmond and then marched south, reaching, by May 15, Wilton, a two-thousand-acre plantation owned by the prominent Randolph family on the James River several miles downstream from the capital. This position, opposite the mouth of Falling Creek, allowed Lafayette to observe the British across the wide river at several important landings and ports, including Warwick, Osborne's and Cary's. Here, he considered his situation "precarious" given the impending union of the forces of Phillips and Cornwallis. Unless he were "speedily and powerfully reinforced," he wrote to General Weedon that day, "there is no chance of resisting the combined armies." At his camp, he lamented, too, that there were more militia "going off than…coming in." He needed riflemen and cavalry or, at the very "least[,] mounted infantry." He implored Weedon, who would soon prove to be one of his most indefatigable subordinates, to send assistance soon, as "it will soon be too late to have it in our power to make a becoming resistance." In a letter to General Wayne from Wilton, he wrote that the Pennsylvanians were needed immediately, by

Wilton, a Randolph family home on the James River used by Lafayette as his headquarters. *Library of Congress.*

a "forced march" if need be. No doubt the marquis would have been pained to know that Wayne's troops were still in Pennsylvania.[96]

On May 18, Lafayette wrote to Greene that the militia being gathered in Virginia to send on to the Carolinas had been retained by state officials, but any Continental levies recently recruited would be sent south, as would supplies procured for Greene's army. He anticipated keeping Wayne's Pennsylvanians with him for a few days "either to strike at Arnold alone, or [to] receive the combined blows of the two armies." In addition to his nine hundred regulars, Lafayette reported that his artillery consisted of four six-pounder guns and two howitzers. The Continentals were augmented by about 1,200 militia in two brigades under Generals Muhlenberg and Nelson. Additionally, General Weedon's militia remained around Fredericksburg, and General Robert Lawson's militia brigade was on the south side of the Appomattox River, although with "very few men" in the ranks.[97]

In the weeks after he had arrived at Richmond, Lafayette had come to recognize that the major weakness of his own force was the lack of cavalry troops. Cautious of the enemy's well-mounted dragoons, Lafayette noted that "we have every thing to fear from their cavalry. They will over run the country and our flanks; our stores, our very camp will be unsecured." Regarding his own cavalrymen from Colonel Charles Armand Tuffin's First Partisan Corps, "ten only are fit for duty"; the rest were "naked, unarmed, dismounted and fatigued to death" while the mounted militias were soon to return home once their tours expired. He had to order Colonel Anthony W. White's thirty-two Continental Light Dragoons, then refitting in the Shenandoah Valley, to remain in Virginia instead of riding to Greene's army, as "we must at least have some patroles."[98] Similarly, Richard Henry Lee, one of Virginia's signers of the Declaration of Independence, wrote to Washington with the same dire assessment a few weeks later. "By seizing the fine horses on James river," he reported, "they have mounted a gallant and most mischievous Cavalry of 5 or 600 in number." And on the same day Lee wrote to Virginia's congressional delegates that the British "have quickly mounted a very formidable Cavalry by seising [sic] on all the fine horses."[99] Unfortunately, as one Virginia leader recognized in June, "this disadvantage in the cavalry cannot be surmounted by the state for want of equipment of which they are very destitute."[100]

Lafayette concentrated his troops at Richmond on May 20, and four days later, he reported officially to Washington from the capital that he was unable to prevent Cornwallis from joining forces with Phillips at Petersburg due to the delay of the Pennsylvania troops. Before Wayne "arrives it is

George Washington, by Charles Willson Peale. *Library of Congress.*

Impossible that 900 Continentals and 40 Horse with a Body of Militia By no Means so Considerable as they were Reported to Be and Whom it is so difficult to Arm, Be with Any Advantage opposed to such a Superiority of forces[,] such a Number of Cavalry to Which May Be added their very prejudicial Command of the Waters." Lafayette continued steps to "remove every valuable property either public or private" at Richmond to keep them from falling into the enemy's hands.[101]

In a private letter to Washington written on the same day, Lafayette shared his reluctance to risk too much against the British given his weak force and reliance on militiamen to augment the strength of his regulars. "A General defeat," he believed, "which with Such a proportion of Militia Must Be Expected would involve this State and our Affairs into Ruin, Has Rendered me Extremely Cautious in My Movements." He also determined not to risk his men defending Richmond, since much of the state's military property had been removed from the city. It would not "be prudent to Expose the troops for the Sake of a few Houses most of which are Empty." He concluded that since he had moved most of the supplies from the town, "this place is a less important object."[102]

Lafayette was also in a quandary over what his course of action should be. "Was I to fight a Battle I'll Be Cut to pieces, the Militia dispersed, and the Arms lost," he wrote, but were he "to decline fighting the Country would think Herself given up." Instead, he determined to "Skarmish" with Cornwallis, "But not to Engage too far, and particularly to take Care against their Immense and excellent Body of Horse, Whom the Militia fears like they would so many wild Beasts."[103]

That night a cautious Lafayette ordered his army's baggage and stores withdrawn from Richmond and moved west. With Cornwallis's force much stronger than his own, he recognized that he was "not Strong Enough even to get Beaten," and until Wayne joined him, "we are Next to Nothing in point of opposition to So Large a force." Keeping his distance from his powerful foe while retiring toward Wayne's expected line of march was Lafayette's prudent course of action.[104]

The Continental forces in Virginia under Lafayette had to be vigorously supported by Virginia if there were any chance of defeating the redcoats. Lafayette implored Jefferson to raise more militia, to repair arms and, especially, to muster light cavalry forces to counter the enemy's superior mounted troops. The marquis urged the governor to seize horses from the citizens, suggesting that "by impressing every fourth Horse, We shou'd be able to raise 200," although properly furnishing and arming dragoons was another challenge. Continuing, he advised Jefferson that "we are in the utmost want of Cavalry; the Enemy's great superiority in Horse giving them such an advantage over us that they have it almost in their power to over run the Country, in spight [sic] of all our efforts." His own cavalry force still numbered just a few dozen mounted and equipped troopers, but the "Enemy have 500 Horse," and Virginia's "mounted Militia are all gone home" taking their accoutrements with them.[105] Virginia authorities, too, understood their military situation. In early June, Benjamin Harrison wrote that "we want arms greatly for infantry, but when we have them it is difficult to find men to use them, all owing to the danger their families are in from the [British] horse."[106]

With a powerful British army at Petersburg and no word from General Wayne, Lafayette faced a difficult situation in late May. Too weak to offer battle to Cornwallis, he nevertheless had to protect American supplies in Virginia and keep up the flagging spirits of the people by maintaining his detachment in the field. Soon, the enemy's actions would force the young French officer to either confront the British redcoats along the James River or avoid a potential defeat by skillful maneuvers. In fact, as Lafayette oversaw the removal of military property from the state's capital, Cornwallis was already on the move toward the Richmond, where he hoped to trap and destroy the rebel defenders.

"LIKE DESPERATE BANDS OF ROBBERS"

Cornwallis Chases Lafayette

Who brought this to pass?
Who has brought the imperial anger?
Who has brought the army with drums and with kettle-drums?
Barbarous kings.
—*"Lament of the Frontier Guard," Rihaku, eighth century*

At the end of May, Lafayette observed new energy in the British camp at Petersburg now that Cornwallis had arrived and assumed command. On the twenty-third, Colonel Tarleton rode north with three hundred dragoons and attacked a party of four hundred militia two miles southwest of Warwick, in Chesterfield County. "Profitting by the very heavy rain," which made firing flintlock muskets almost impossible, Tarleton's men surprised the Patriots, killed several and took forty to fifty prisoners. Some of the militiamen "were cut very barbarously" by the enemy's saber-wielding cavalrymen, Lafayette reported to Wayne. Tarleton learned from the captives that Lafayette's main force was posted between Richmond and Wilton.[107]

Lafayette soon heard that Cornwallis left Petersburg on May 24 and marched east to Maycox, a plantation on the south side of the river in Prince George County. The two-story manor house, owned by David Meade, was "a commodious brick dwelling house" across from Westover and was known for its extensive gardens. Here, beginning on May 24, Cornwallis spent most of the next three days crossing his army over to

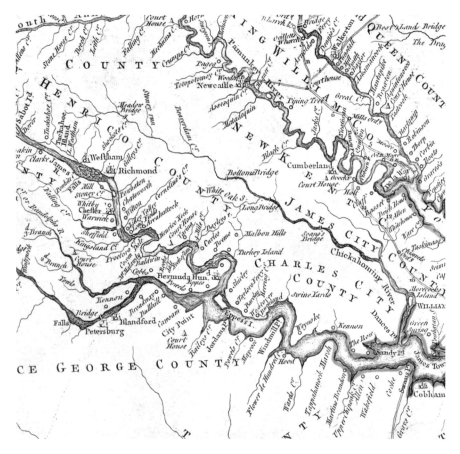

The area from the British crossing of the James at Maycox to Hanover Court House (top of map). *North Carolina Collection, University of North Carolina–Chapel Hill.*

"a fertile quarter of Virginia," wrote Tarleton, to enable "the British to prosecute such operations against the Americans as future circumstances should render eligible." The troops, horses, wagons and artillery crossed by boats constructed under General Arnold's direction and were of "great utility." By the twenty-sixth, Cornwallis was on the same side of the river as Lafayette's weaker force and had hundreds of cavalry troops capable of quick strikes against the rebels.[108]

Lafayette advised Jefferson that without Wayne's expected reinforcements "in our present situation I dare hardly risk the smallest matter." Rather, he could only hope to "check Ld. Cornwallis, without giving him an opportunity of ingaging [*sic*] us further than we wish, or than prudence will justify." This would be the marquis' modus operandi for several months, until his army grew in numbers. On the afternoon of the twenty-sixth, Lafayette rode north of Richmond to reconnoiter Brook's Bridge on Upham Brook, an upper tributary of the Chickahominy River, "as He has sent in Orders to move on the Troops to that place," away from Cornwallis, whose soldiers were then moving north from Westover.[109]

At Westover, Cornwallis met two thousand well-equipped reinforcements recently arrived from New York and transported up the James River. He dispatched the Seventeenth Foot, two battalions of Hessians and several other companies to return to Portsmouth and retained all other units for his own operations. Benedict Arnold also left Cornwallis's camp at this point to return to New York and eventual obscurity in London.[110]

White Oak Swamp, where British troops camped before marching to Newcastle. *Library of Congress.*

While preparing to continue his march from Westover the next day, Cornwallis wrote to Clinton in New York on May 26. "If offensive war is intended," he posited, "Virginia appears to me to be the only province in which it can be carried on," but he warned that to keep it in British hands would require "a considerable army." He modestly denied seeking command of such a force for himself and reiterated his conclusion that the backcountry could not be firmly held anywhere in the South "against a persevering enemy in a country where we have no water communication and where few of the inhabitants are active or useful friends." He would discover this for himself over the next several weeks as his fast-moving army spread out across central Virginia.

Cornwallis initially considered trying "to dislodge La Fayette from Richmond and with my light troops to destroy any magazines or stores in the neighborhood" and then march east toward Williamsburg, "where some subsistence can be procured" for his men and horses.[111] However, he soon altered these plans. Reinforced, the British commander ordered his regiments to march west to the bridge at Turkey Island Creek, just south of Malvern Hill, a plantation in southeastern Henrico County. From this stream, the British advanced north on May 27 to White Oak Swamp and camped on its southern edge for a night. On the following day, the redcoats passed around the eastern side of the marsh and halted at Bottoms Bridge on the Chickahominy River on the Williamsburg Road. A smaller column of British soldiers marched east of Malvern Hill, crossed the Chickahominy at Long Bridge and then rejoined Cornwallis's troops the next day.[112]

Cornwallis's passage of the James and quick movement north from Westover convinced Lafayette that Richmond was no longer tenable.[113] Jefferson also recognized the dire military situation the state faced. Prior to Lafayette's evacuating the capital, Jefferson wrote to General Washington on May 28. He reported that the British had been reinforced at Westover and turned toward Richmond, where the "Marquis Fayette lay with 3000 Men, regulars and militia, that being the whole number we could Arm till the arrival of the 1100 Arms from Rhode Island." The governor was concerned that even if Cornwallis had "no opportunity of annihilating the Marquis's Army," he would be able to keep Lafayette at bay while part of the British invaders devastated "an unarmed Country and…[led] the minds of the people to acquiescence under those events which they see no human power prepared to ward off." Jefferson asked Washington to "lend us your personal aid," noting that his appearance "among [the people] I say would restore full confidence of salvation and would render them equal to whatever is not

Cornwallis and Lafayette both camped their troops around Malvern Hill in eastern Henrico County near the James River. *Library of Congress.*

impossible." He flattered the general by saying that if Washington were to come to Virginia to defend his native land, it would be difficult to "keep men out of the field," and he assured Washington that many "members of weight in our legislature" concurred with his sentiments.[114]

The philosopher of Monticello was not the only man in Virginia during the British invasions of 1781 who sought Washington's presence in the commonwealth. Some Virginians considered appointing an executive with extraordinary powers, due to the state's inability to organize an effective defense. In early June, assembly delegate George Nicholas "gave notice that he shou'd this day move to have a Dictator appointed," with Washington and General Greene "talk'd of."[115] A witness to the assembly's session wrote that Nicholas favored installing "a Dictator…in this Commonwealth who should have the power of disposing of the lives and fortunes of the Citizens thereof without being subject to account." He suggested George Washington for this office, citing "the practice of the Romans on similar occasions." Reports claimed Patrick Henry supported this motion. Jefferson was convinced that Henry sought the dictatorial role for himself, but none of Henry's own writings confirm this. The motion, in the end, was defeated, although Jefferson reported that "it wanted a few votes only of being passed."[116]

Virginia signer of the Declaration of Independence Richard Henry Lee complained about his state's inability to defend itself against the British in 1781. *Library of Congress.*

Similarly, Richard Henry Lee held that "the remedy best fitted, and most likely to baffle the designs of our enemies and to secure the liberty of this country" was "in the popularity, the judgment, and the experience of Gen. Washington." He went on to the state's delegates in Congress:

Let Congress send him immediately to Virginia, and as the head of the Fœderal Union let them possess the General with Dictatorial power until the general Assembly can be convened, and have determined upon his powers, and let it be recommended to the Assembly when met to continue this power for 6, 8, or 10 months as the case may require...the present necessity not only justifies but absolutely demands the measure...There is no time to be lost gentlemen in this business, for the enemy are pushing their present advantages with infinite diligence and art.

The letter expressed the frustration among the state's Patriots at Cornwallis's unimpeded movements and the government's ineptitude at opposing him.[117]

Even if the commanding general were to come immediately to Virginia to assume command of its defenses as Jefferson and others urged, the British threat to the commonwealth was more immediate than the eventual presence of Washington could counter. In response, Jefferson called out additional militia troops from the state's western frontier communities for tours of two months. It was "necessary for us to bring a very great Force into the Field" to battle Cornwallis's troops, Jefferson announced, so "let every man who possibly can, come armed with a good rifle and those who cannot must bring a good smooth Bore if they have it." The governor advised the backcountry militia officers that until "the Reinforcements now called for get into the Field the whole Country lies open to a most powerful Army headed by the most active, enterprising and vindictive Officer who has ever appeared in Arms against us." Time would soon prove the accuracy of his description of Cornwallis.[118]

Once Cornwallis's redcoats were established north of the James, American troops were on the move to avoid a confrontation with them. After leaving Richmond, Lafayette marched his men along the Fredericksburg Road over Brook's Bridge and then led them northwest via Winston's Bridge (or another nearby crossing) on the upper Chickahominy River.[119]

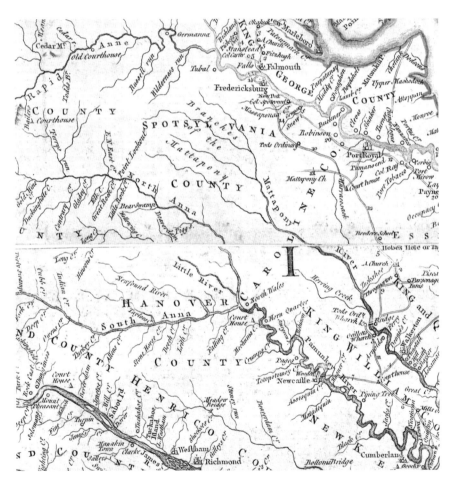

Central Virginia, in which Lafayette maneuvered to avoid Cornwallis's army. *North Carolina Collection, University of North Carolina–Chapel Hill.*

By May 28, Lafayette's troops were positioned near Gold Mine Creek at the plantation of Colonel Nathaniel West Dandridge, father-in-law of Patrick Henry. This well-known site was usually referred to in wartime letters merely as "Dandridge's" and was located between Gold Mine and Allen's Creeks south of the South Anna River in western Hanover County. With few towns in the Piedmont region of Revolutionary War–era Virginia, extensive plantations such as Colonel Dandridge's offered eighteenth-century armies fields for encampments, springs and creeks for fresh water, forage for horses and access to road networks. This location also put Lafayette at a safe distance from the British, who were at the time close to the Pamunkey River in eastern Hanover County.

From Dandridge's, Lafayette reported to Jefferson on May 28 that the British appeared to be headed toward Fredericksburg. Cornwallis was intent on destroying the valuable iron foundry and small arms factory called Rappahannock Forge, operated by James Hunter and located nearby at Falmouth, on the north bank of the Rappahannock River in Stafford County.[120] This extensive producer of arms and equipment was crucial to Virginia's war efforts, as one of Jefferson's correspondents, James Mercer, made clear the previous month:

I am sure I need not tell you that it is from Mr. Hunter's works that every camp kettle has been supplied for the continental and all other troops employed in this State and to the Southward this year past: that all anchors for this State and Maryland and some for [the] continent have been procured from the same works; that without these works we have no other resource for these articles and that without the assistance of bar iron made there even the planters hereabouts and to the Southward of this place would not be able to make bread to eat. As to the Town [of Fredericksburg] itself I need not inform you that the public manufactory of Arms is here—that without it, all our Arms, however so little injured wou'd be useless to us; besides the number of new muskets & bayonets made there, renders that an object worthy our preserving & the Enemy's destruction—To this however, I may add that there is not one spot in the State so generally useful in our military operations [a] full one-third of all new lines rendezvous here; all the Troops from North to South & South to North must pass through this Town, where wagons are repaired, horses shoed and many other &c which they cou'd not proceed on without, the Troops get provisions here to the next Stage & no place is so convenient to a very extensive & productive Country for the reception of Grain & other Articles of Provision. If this state of facts is admitted, can it be doubted but that the

Enemy will consider it as one of their first objects to deprive us of so many advantages to their prejudice.

Several years earlier, Governor Patrick Henry also recognized the importance of Hunter's works, stating "there was no Manufactory of Iron in this State which was carried on to such an extent, and to Purposes of such vast Importance as Mr. Hunter's near Fredericksburg."[121] Hunter advised Jefferson on May 30 that with Tarleton's troops moving closer to his factory and mills, "at present, I am removing my Tools, and a [putting] total stoppage to every thing."[122]

The marquis heard reports that Tarleton's dragoons were at Hanover Court House on the twenty-eighth, which supported his conclusion that the enemy was headed north. Lafayette needed to keep another river between his detachment and the enemy, and if the reports of cavalry at Hanover Court House were true, he had to move farther north. "Our small corps moves this evening towards Andersons Bridge," he continued, referring to a wooden span over the North Anna River leading into western Caroline County. "We shall be upon a parallel line with the Enemy keeping the upper part of the Country," he noted, which would also bring him closer to Wayne's anticipated route.[123]

Once again, Lafayette complained that "all the fine Horses in the Country are falling into the Enemy's hands" since Virginians were slow to move them out of the invaders' path. "This will in the end prove a ruin to this State," he predicted, adding that "the British have so many Dragoons that it becomes impossible either to stop or reconnoitre their movements, and much more so to send impressing parties around their Camp" for horses and supplies. Jefferson was to an extent limited in his power to find mounts, as the law only allowed him to confiscate horses within twenty miles of the army, "and unless the executive give a warrant for 50 miles we cannot get a single Horse." Lafayette later recalled that although he tried to keep a safe distance from Cornwallis's invaders, the enemy's cavalry was a constant threat: "For a long time we had Tarleton entering our camp two hours after it was abandoned." Moreover, Lafayette had "no Riflemen, no Cavalry, no arms, and few Militia coming. I wish Your Excellency will order Riflemen to join us. Without them and without Horse we can do nothing."[124]

By the time Lafayette wrote this letter to Jefferson, the governor was already at Monticello, his mountaintop home overlooking Charlottesville, near the base of the Blue Ridge Mountains. The state's legislators had left Richmond due to the danger from the British invaders and planned to

Monticello, the home of Thomas Jefferson, was raided by Tarleton's dragoons. The image shows it as it appeared several years after the Revolutionary War. *Library of Congress.*

reconvene on May 24 at Charlottesville, seventy miles west. Jefferson had been pressuring the assembly for some recourse on procuring horses and optimistically advised Lafayette on May 29 that once the state's upper house convened, "I believe they are disposed to strengthen you with Cavalry to any Amount you think proper and with as good Horses as you shall think Oeconomy should induce us to take." Jefferson was careful to remind his correspondent that if he resorted to impressing horses, the sensibilities of the local owners must be kept in mind: army "officers of mild and condescending Tempers and manners [should be] employed and particularly instructed while they prosecute their Object steadily to use every soothing Art possible" to avoid alienating the people. To encourage the marquis, Jefferson predicted that the western militia would come to aid him soon but was unrealistic when he wrote that Lafayette "shall be sufficiently reinforced and be able to engage [Cornwallis] on your own terms. This may be the Case when your Superiority in Cavalry shall become decided which I have the most sanguine hopes the Assembly will immediately provide for."[125]

On May 29, still with headquarters at Dandridge's, Lafayette wrote to General Wayne. He predicted Cornwallis would "push for Fredericksburg" and that his Continentals would move there, too, ahead of the enemy. "I

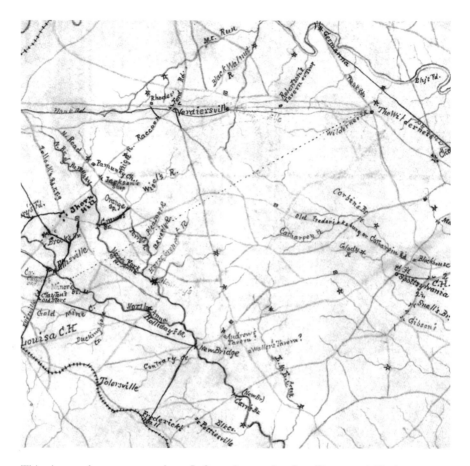

This nineteenth-century map shows Lafayette's campsites from Davenport's Ford to Wilderness Run, as well as Ely's and Raccoon Fords. Brock's Bridge is also shown on the left. *Library of Congress.*

request," wrote the marquis, that "you will leave your baggage behind and come by forced marches," so as to "form a junction as soon as possible." Without these reinforcements, Lafayette remained powerless to stop the British advance.[126]

From Dandridge's, Lafayette's force again moved north, crossed the South Anna River at Ground Squirrel Bridge and reached Scotchtown, a large frame house previously owned by Virginia's former governor, Patrick Henry. Farther on, the troops halted to encamp on May 30 at Anderson's Bridge on the North Anna River and then moved the next day into Caroline County by wading Davenport's Ford several miles downstream rather than crossing at the bridge. Still keeping his distance from the enemy to the east, he advised

Patrick Henry's former home, Scotchtown, in Hanover County was passed by both armies during the 1781 campaign. *Library of Congress.*

Lafayette's small army crossed the North Anna River at Davenport's Ford, near modern Beaverdam. *Author photograph.*

Jefferson (in a letter intercepted by British mounted scouts) that he was working to gather militia troops with his own soldiers and expected to meet General Weedon's Virginia militia brigade from around Fredericksburg the next day. Since "the enemy have 500 horse and we 40," he stayed west of the Piedmont rivers' fall line, getting closer to Wayne. Regarding Cornwallis to the east, he quipped, "My Lord [Cornwallis] is going from his friends, and we are going to meet ours."[127]

Passing through a sparsely inhabited countryside in southern Spotsylvania County, the American column by June 1 had reached Mattaponi Church, once located on a hilltop just north of the Ta River, near its confluence with the Mat River. This frame church, no longer standing, stood on the east side of the road, about five miles south of the current Spotsylvania Court House. Not to be confused with the old Mattaponi Anglican Church in King and Queen County, it was built in 1725 and was probably "sixty feet long and twenty-four feet wide, of wood construction with brick underpinning." Although no evidence of a structure or graveyard exists today, and archaeology work in the late 1970s failed to find evidence of the building, it is shown on several eighteenth-century maps, although by the 1860s, it

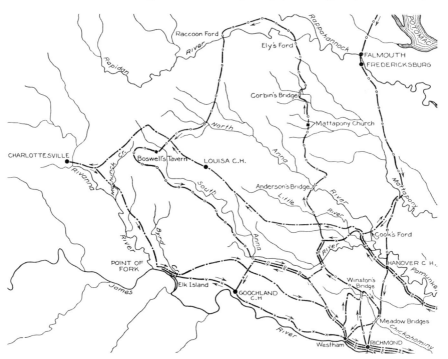

Map of Lafayette's route to the Rapidan River and Raccoon Ford. *Landers*, Yorktown, 1781.

seems this chapel was no longer standing. Here, Lafayette camped overnight and may have been joined by part of Weeden's militiamen.[128]

Traveling over flat, sandy roads on the night of June 1, the marquis pushed his men about twelve miles farther to Corbin's Bridge, where they encamped along the sluggish Po River. Although their exact route to this location is not recorded, the column of Continentals and militiamen probably marched on the south side of the Po River from Mattaponi Church to the bridge since the troops subsequently proceeded to the Brock Road, north of the Po. Lafayette's position put him near enough to Fredericksburg to defend the town if he so desired and north of several small rivers in case Cornwallis advanced quickly against him.[129] The Frenchman was still anxious about his lack of cavalry, which prevented him from knowing Cornwallis's exact location. He surmised that the British might head west from Hanover along the James River rather than

Map detail depicting key sites on Lafayette's line of march, from Corbin's Bridge (lower right) to Wilderness Bridge (center) and Ely's Ford (top). *Library of Congress.*

pursue him, but the "enemy's immense superiority on cavalry makes it impossible to know their true intentions."[130]

At this time, Lafayette received a June 1 letter from General Weedon at Fredericksburg. Although Weedon reported great difficulties in dispersing supplies from area depots to prevent the British from capturing them and for "the salvation of this town," he did report that 250 men of the militia of Stafford and King George Counties were assembling at Hunter's Iron Works. He was trying to arm them and was "obligated to attend every department" at the town amid "very great confusion." A few days later, Weedon reported that he had been able to move out of Fredericksburg all stores, except for some corn meal and forage, due to a lack of wagons. He tried to impress some wagons from local inhabitants, but the militia detachments assigned to do so were ineffective in the task. The marquis directed Weedon to have his men join the army immediately, and it appears that militia from Caroline and Spotsylvania Counties joined Lafayette about this time. Weedon expected additional men from Prince William County to arrive soon, though they were largely unarmed.[131]

From Corbin's Bridge, Lafayette's small army plodded several miles east on June 3 and then turned north on the Brock Road. Crossing several small creeks, the troops halted later that day on the southeast side of Wilderness Run, where a bridge crossed the small stream in a wide valley. Opposite the location of the preserved nineteenth-century house called Ellwood, the marquis had his soldiers camp in the open fields along the run while he considered crossing the nearby Rapidan River a few miles to his north and tried to learn of Wayne's progress into Virginia.[132]

Site of Lafayette's army encampment at Wilderness Run, south of the Rapidan. *Author photograph.*

While on the march to the Rapidan through the forests of the Virginia countryside, Lafayette received intelligence regarding Lord Cornwallis's movements, which were "not as yet well explained." Much of the information reaching the American camp was conflicting and incomplete. The enemy still appeared to be headed for Fredericksburg, but Lafayette advised General Greene that the military stores and all removable property at Hunter's Rappahannock Forge had been sent away. As it happened, while Lafayette rested his footsore troops beside Wilderness Run, Cornwallis and his junior officers were in the midst of aggressive operations to strike at Virginia's supply collections west of Richmond. Lafayette's supposition made on June 3—"it is possible they mean to make a stroke towards Charlottesville"—proved to be correct, for the British were moving west in three columns to destroy rebel supply caches, scatter the state's militiamen and, in a lighting strike, capture Virginia's chief executive, Thomas Jefferson.[133]

Lafayette's retrograde movements north from Richmond to the Rapidan were made due to the vigorous conduct of Cornwallis's advance once his soldiers crossed the James at Westover. On his way east to Bottoms Bridge on the Chickahominy River, Cornwallis was apprised of Lafayette's abandonment of Richmond and his movement to the north. The British commander therefore decided not to march his men to Williamsburg and also elected to bypass the new Virginia capital. Instead, after his army's brief halt at Bottoms Bridge, Cornwallis led his redcoats, Hessians and provincials to the Pamunkey River, northeast of Richmond, to destroy valuable enemy property as he chased Lafayette's smaller command.

At this time, Cornwallis supposedly wrote to General Clinton (in a letter allegedly intercepted by Patriot forces but missing from Cornwallis's existing correspondence) that "the boy cannot escape me," referring to the young marquis. However, the authenticity of this statement is questionable and may have been a phrase originating with Clinton in a letter to Lord Germain. One of Lafayette's major biographers, Louis Gottschalk, discounted the anecdote and pointed out that it may have first appeared in David Ramsey's history of the Revolutionary War in the South, published in 1793. Nevertheless, it has been repeated by unquestioning writers since the early nineteenth century.[134]

During the Revolutionary era, eastern Hanover County along the Pamunkey River was a thriving area of commercial activity, as planters brought their hogsheads of tobacco to warehouses and wharves on the riverbanks for shipment abroad by the many factors, brokers and merchant ships plying the Tidewater's navigable estuaries. This trade is nonexistent today, but two centuries ago, the small river ports east of Richmond were attractive targets to British officers looking to cripple Virginia's economy and wherewithal to fight the war for independence. Cornwallis recognized the value of these ports and set his army on a course to destroy them.

At Bottoms Bridge on May 28, the British crossed the meandering Chickahominy and marched north to Newcastle, a village on the south bank of the Pamunkey River, which they reached on May 29. It was "a small town with very few houses, situated on high ground," according to a French officer in 1781. The troops probably followed several roads on their march, first to Old Church and then to the river at Broaddus Flats, a wide plain south of the Pamunkey. In its most active period of the mid-eighteenth century, Newcastle included fifty-two lots, six lanes parallel to the river and three streets ending at the water, which was spanned by a bridge twelve feet wide. Prior to the war, a number of Scottish factors had established warehouses and wharves there for handling agricultural commodities. Upon their arrival, the British destroyed tobacco and other property at the storehouses and were joined here by a cavalry detachment of the Queen's Rangers under Colonel Simcoe that had marched on Cornwallis's eastern flank from Malvern Hill.[135]

Simcoe later wrote that during this march, his troopers were the rear guard of Cornwallis's column and provided valuable service. He noted that

> *the rear was uncommonly long and the road running in many places, through thickets, patroles of the enemy might easily have taken a great many stragglers. He* [Simcoe] *divided his cavalry into small parties, left them at different distances, and collected the tired men as well as possible, which was not in the power of the infantry, that formed the rear guard to effect.*[136]

The British force, preceded in its northward march by Tarleton's dragoons, hiked farther along the south bank of the Pamunkey to destroy more stores and tobacco at Hanover Town, a busy port founded in 1672 and also known as Page's Warehouse. A bridge spanned the river here to King William County. A French officer wrote later in 1781 that "Cornwallis had the fine warehouses burned, as well as several private houses whose owners were suspected of devotion to the cause of independence." The town consisted of several blocks, with an open square in the center, and the warehouses were presumably close to the waterfront.[137]

As the mounted troops ranged from the column to destroy and loot rebel property, the British army continued its relentless incursion to Hanover

Hanover County Court House, occupied briefly by Cornwallis's soldiers pursuing Lafayette, is still in use today. *Library of Congress.*

Court House, which it reached on May 30. There was "a very fine and large inn" at this hamlet, known as the Shelton Tavern, once owned by the parents of Patrick Henry's wife, Sarah Shelton. Additionally, the public buildings included a handsome brick arcaded courthouse, built around 1735, and still in use today. Nearby, the British discovered ten French-made twenty-four-pounder cannons that were too large for the redcoats to remove, so they spiked and threw five or six of them into the Pamunkey. These guns were too heavy to be used as field pieces, so presumably Virginia authorities intended them to be used for fortifications or batteries elsewhere in the state.[138]

Cornwallis's rapid advance caused much alarm among civilians in central Virginia and the Tidewater. "Distressing is the scene displayed by the inhabitants who are flying with their families," General Weedon reported to Lafayette on June 4. One of Virginia's congressmen noted in mid-June that the enemy's superior cavalry allowed it to "range about the country as to dismay the people not a little and keep them in continual alarm for the safety of their families." Likewise, Assemblyman Benjamin Harrison wrote that "we are in the most distressed condition from the sea to the Mountains."[139]

Summarizing the enemy's outrages in an early July letter, James Madison wrote that

> *no description can give you an adequate idea of the barbarity with which the Enemy have conducted the war in the Southern States. Every outrage*

76

which humanity could suffer has been committed by them. Desolation rather than conquest seems to have been their object. They have acted more like desperate bands of Robbers or Buccaneers than like a nation making war for dominion. Negroes, Horses, Tobacco &c not the standards and arms of their antagonists are the trophies which display their success. Rapes, murders & the whole catalogue of individual cruelties, not protection & the distribution of justice are the acts which characterize the [sphere] of their usurped Jurisdiction.

Madison concluded that "it is much to be regretted that these things are so little known in Europe. Were they published to the World in their true colours, the British nation would be hated by all nations as much as they have heretofore been feared by any."[140]

About this time, Tarleton's cavalrymen sacked the Hanover home of the recently widowed Elizabeth Clay, whose four-year-old son, Henry, would later move to Kentucky and gain fame as a Speaker of the U.S. House of Representatives, presidential candidate and U.S. secretary of state. At the Clays' farm east of Ashland in an area called "the Slashes," dragoons pillaged the house, taking food and liquor and destroying valuable furniture and clothing inside—including Mrs. Clay's wedding dress. Most of the family's slaves left with the British, who reportedly desecrated the graves of her husband and mother with their bayonets.[141]

Still moving northward, Cornwallis led the main part of his army north from Hanover Court House, as Simcoe's dragoons chased and captured a small party of Virginia militia at the South Anna Bridge.[142] The British moved along the south bank of the North Anna River to a crossing of that river a dozen miles or so to the northwest. By this time, Cornwallis had advanced his invading army to a point only thirty-five miles from Fredericksburg, leaving behind him a path of destroyed military supplies, burned tobacco and looted rebel homes. The redcoat general now faced a decision regarding how to continue his campaign to subdue Virginia. Lafayette's rebel force still eluded him, but the British had been largely successful in their devastation of the enemy's means to wage war. By the first few days of June, his lordship would decide to refocus his operations in a manner that would bring even more chaos and destruction to the Old Dominion.[143]

5

"WITH RAPID AND DEVIOUS MOVEMENTS"

The British Strike West

Let your plans be dark and impenetrable as night, and when you move, fall like a thunderbolt.
—*Sun Tzu,* The Art of War, *sixth century BC*

On June 1, Cornwallis's troops arrived at Tile's Ordinary near Cook's Ford on the North Anna,[144] where they bivouacked along the river's steep banks for several days. The cavalry ranged north of the river to Chesterfield Tavern and Bowling Green looking for enemy supplies, horses and intelligence. From Bowling Green, Rappahannock Forge was only twenty miles from Tarleton's dragoons, but the British cavalry commander apparently made no further progress toward Fredericksburg.[145]

At Cook's Ford (later called Ox Ford), Cornwallis contemplated his next move. Thirty miles to the north, Fredericksburg was an inviting target, not only for the rebel arms manufactory located nearby but also because the town was a significant commercial center at the fall line of the Rappahannock River. Possession of the town and destruction of the military materiel there would hamper Virginia's ability to support General Greene's army in South Carolina and undermine the state's ability to defend itself.

The British commander, however, decided not to continue his advance toward Fredericksburg. Cornwallis reasoned that Fredericksburg could be captured more efficiently by a naval expedition from the lower Chesapeake, and he was no longer convinced that it was worth the effort to move there

Remnant of an eighteenth-century road leading to Cook's Ford on the south side of the North Anna River, where the British camped for several days in June. *Author photograph.*

by additional days of marching through the heat of Virginia's late spring. "From what I could learn of the present state of Hunter's Iron Manufactory it did not appear of so much importance as the stores on the other side of the country," he concluded. He was also concerned about Lafayette's intentions as well. With his superior cavalry units, Cornwallis probably knew of Lafayette's position at Corbin's Bridge during the first few days of June and was aware that the marquis' small but growing force of Continentals and militia soldiers were positioned to his northwest. He also recognized that the farther north he pushed Lafayette's army, the closer the marquis got to Wayne's Continentals marching south from Pennsylvania, which would significantly increase the Americans' strength. Given Lafayette's skillful handling of his troops to avoid a risky battle, Cornwallis doubted he could prevent him from joining Wayne. Far from his own source of supplies at Portsmouth and with an army that had marched hundreds of miles since leaving Wilmington in late April, Cornwallis elected not to proceed farther north from Cook's Ford.[146]

Instead, his lordship decided to make a rapid movement to the west, where he knew Virginia and Continental authorities had collected much of their military stores. As an experienced campaigner, the British general perceived that although Lafayette had been able to avoid a pitched battle by maneuvering just out of reach of the more numerous royal army, by moving so far north the young Frenchman had "uncovered" rebel logistical depots to the west, which were guarded by few Patriot forces. In a report to Clinton, Cornwallis wrote that the time had now come to take "advantage of the Marquis's passing the Rappahannock [River]." By turning to his left, Cornwallis and his troops were poised to exploit this favorable situation, a maneuver they initiated on June 2.[147]

Military caches, however, would not be the only targets for the British host. On May 10, the Virginia legislature had adjourned in Richmond, "the movements of the enemy in the neighbourhood of this place not admitting of that quiet necessary to the Deliberations of Public Bodies," Governor Jefferson reported. Instead, the delegates "determined to meet at Charlottesville on the 24th" of the month.[148] Jefferson left Richmond on May 15, stopping to join his family in eastern Goochland County at Tuckahoe Plantation along the River Road, an early 1700s Randolph family home where he had spent much of his early youth and received his initial education. He then made his way to Monticello with his family over the next few days.[149]

Only two of the governor's Executive Council members arrived in Charlottesville to meet on May 24, so a quorum was not made. Assemblymen had to seek lodgings in the small town and the surrounding countryside at plantation homes and rustic inns. A delegate from Botetourt County wrote that "we all fixed ourselves very comfortably, in full assurance of being unmolested by the enemy." On May 28, there were enough members of the assembly gathered to convene a proper legislative session. Senate leader Archibald Cary and House of Delegates Speaker Benjamin Harrison were

Tuckahoe is where Jefferson joined his family after leaving Richmond. *Library of Congress.*

both present, as well as houseguests of the governor at Monticello. Virginia militia general Thomas Nelson Jr. also lodged at Jefferson's Albemarle home, then under construction.[150]

The House took up much war-related business, such as allowing (with some restrictions) Lafayette to impress horses from citizens in "counties contiguous to the march of the enemy," to keep them from falling into British hands. The delegates also resolved that Jefferson immediately order enough militia into service as would enable Lafayette to "oppose the enemy with effect" and to raise additional cavalry troops for service with the marquis. On June 1, the house asked Jefferson to "call for the immediate assistance of Brigadier General [Daniel] Morgan," a Virginia officer living in the lower Shenandoah Valley who had won the Battle of Cowpens, South Carolina, in January 1781. Morgan was to muster and take command of all men he could recruit for three months service to reinforce Lafayette's army.[151]

Surely on Jefferson's mind during these last few days of May was the fact that his term as the commonwealth's governor would come to an end on June 2, a date he anticipated with relief. The legislature, however, named June 2 as the day it would choose a new governor, but since that date fell on a Saturday, the election was rescheduled to June 4—three days after Jefferson's term officially expired. The House journal for June 2 includes a telling entry indicating how close the British threat had come to Charlottesville: "Resolved, that in case the enemy shall be in possession of this place on Monday next, this House do adjourn to Penn's Ordinary [in northern Amherst County]." Dramatic events would soon transpire in Charlottesville and central Virginia to make an election on June 4 impossible and contribute to confusion, indecision and a stain on Jefferson's reputation that he spent years trying to erase.[152]

The House journal for June 4, 1781, recorded only two resolutions that day and no other business. The first matter mentioned the "present dangerous invasion" by Cornwallis and decreed that only forty delegates would be required during the alarm "to proceed upon business" of the state. The second resolution adjourned the house until June 7, when the assembly would reconvene at Staunton, thirty-five miles west across the Blue Ridge Mountains. Immediately thereafter, the legislators began to hurriedly leave Charlottesville to avoid what Speaker Harrison called "an implacable enemy...now roaming at large in the very bowels of our country."[153]

The delegates' haste was not unwarranted. Within hours, British dragoons and foot soldiers were tearing through the streets of Charlottesville looking to capture the state's governor and its assemblymen—not all of whom managed to escape.

The "implacable" British were indeed coming. Cornwallis's superiority over Lafayette in mounted forces enabled him to obtain valuable information about the movements of his wily foe during May 1781. British dragoons managed to capture American couriers riding along Virginia's roads and glean useful information about Lafayette's army and the rebel government. Thus, from an intercepted dispatch, Cornwallis knew of the state legislature's relocation to Charlottesville and the locations of Patriot supply depots west of Richmond. "Earl Cornwallis had clear intelligence of the meeting of the governor and assembly at Charlottesville," Tarleton recalled, and also knew that von Steuben commanded several hundred Continental Army recruits at Point of Fork, a supply depot and training camp at the confluence of the James and Rivanna Rivers. Thus, at Cook's Ford on June 2, the British commander abandoned his pursuit of Lafayette and his march toward Fredericksburg in favor of moving west, to focus his attention on striking key logistical points and Virginia's civil government.[154]

Cornwallis's plan was to use his superior mounted troops under Colonels Simcoe and Tarleton in two quick raids to destroy the rebel stockpiles at Old Albemarle Courthouse and Point of Fork, both situated on the north side of

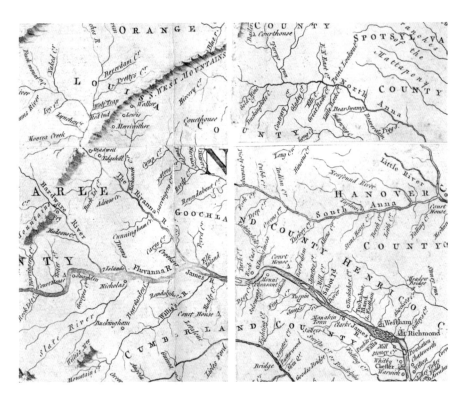

The region between Richmond and Charlottesville is where Cornwallis, Tarleton and Simcoe marched west. Point of Fork is just west of Elk Island. *North Carolina Collection, University of North Carolina–Chapel Hill.*

the James River. His troopers would also strike Charlottesville in order to capture Governor Jefferson, interrupt the state legislature and burn any supplies they found there. Preceded by a "cloud of light troops," the general and his foot regiments were to follow the cavalry columns at a slower pace and eventually rendezvous at a position along the James near Point of Fork. Cornwallis ordered that the two columns should strike their objectives "at the same moment"; then the cavalry would reunite with the main British force.[155]

In order to strengthen Tarleton's force of 180 dragoons, Cornwallis ordered a detachment of the Second Battalion of the Seventy-first Regiment to provide seventy men to ride on the backs of some of the legion's mounts. This assignment angered the Seventy-first Foot's officers, who held Tarleton responsible for the heavy casualties suffered by the regiment's First Battalion at the Battle of Cowpens, South Carolina, in January. In light of this heated dissention, Cornwallis assigned the Twenty-third Regiment, the Royal Welch Fusiliers, to provide the additional men. Thus, although some officers were evidently hostile toward the young Tarleton, Cornwallis obviously seems not to have doubted the young dragoon's ability to command and operate independently in the field.[156]

On the rainy morning of June 3, Tarleton's force rode west from Cook's Ford along the right bank of the North Anna to Benjamin Brown's Ordinary in western Hanover County, two miles south of Davenport's Ford, where Lafayette had crossed his army several days earlier. From here, the troopers rode south, passing "Scotchtown" before proceeding to Ground Squirrel Bridge, situated on what was commonly called the Mountain Road. Turning west to follow the Mountain Road into Louisa County, the skies had cleared and he rested his troops and their mounts around noon due to the heat.[157]

By the late afternoon, the column started westward again and, after dark, reached Cuckoo Tavern, where the troopers and horses halted again for water and refreshment after a twenty-two-mile ride. As Tarleton and some of his officers relaxed inside the tavern, they were observed by Captain John "Jack" Jouett Jr., an observant young militia officer from Charlottesville. Jouett either overheard the enemy officers discussing their mission or guessed where such a large detachment of cavalry must be bound. Around 10:00 p.m., he slipped away from the tavern, unnoticed, in order to warn Jefferson and the legislators in Charlottesville of the impending danger.[158]

Assuming that the British cavalry would ride to Charlottesville on the main road through Louisa Court House, Jouett jumped on his horse and sped west on a little-used trail south of and parallel to Tarleton's route. Despite the claims of some earlier writers, it remains unknown which road Jouett took to warn the governor. The Three Notched (or Chopt) Road was too far south for Jouett to utilize if he hoped to reach Monticello before the enemy, so he must have ridden on a road north of it. He might have traveled on a rough path between the Mountain Road and the Three Notched Road and then entered the latter near Boyd Tavern or Shadwell in eastern Albemarle County.

Jouett eventually turned south off the Three Notched Road and crossed the Rivanna River at Milton, four miles east of Monticello. He galloped up the wooded slopes to warn the governor of the approaching British force just before daybreak on June 4. Jefferson later recalled that Jouett knew the "byways of the neighborhood, passed the enemy's encampment, rode all night, and before sunrise of…[June 4] called at Monticello." Next, Jouett sped down into Charlottesville to warn the assemblymen in town, many of whom were staying at Swan Tavern, owned by his father.[159] "Had it not been

Milton Ford on the Rivanna River was used by Jack Jouett on his hurried ride to Monticello. *Author photograph.*

for the extraordinary exertions of a young gentleman who discovered their intentions and got round them in the night," wrote House Speaker Harrison, "not one man of those in town would have escaped" the enemy. Harrison also reported that "so incredulous were some of us" to Jouett's warning "that it was with much difficulty they could be prevailed to adjourn."[160]

While Jouett raced through the murky woods, Tarleton led his column to Louisa Court House, which he reached at 11:00 p.m. on the third, and then "remained on a plentiful plantation till two o'clock in the morning, at which time he resumed his march." The British rode eleven miles west from the courthouse village to Boswell's Tavern, built in 1735 and owned by Colonel John Boswell, a native Scot. Here Tarleton's men burned "twelve wagons that were on their journey, under a weak guard, from the upper parts of Virginia and Maryland, with arms and clothing for the Continental troops in South Carolina."[161]

Tarleton's swift-moving column terrified many area civilians. A young York County refugee named Eliza J. Ambler wrote of her family's plight as Tarleton's cavalry rode through Louisa County, where she had sought safety. "We only had time to learn that they were on the road from Richmond, when we were again in the carriage," trying to avoid the enemy. She worried

Boswell's Tavern in western Louisa County is where Tarleton burned rebel wagons and Lafayette later encamped. *Library of Congress.*

for the safety of her father, treasurer of Virginia Jacquelin Ambler, as the "public office which he holds makes it absolutely necessary for him to run no risks of falling into the hands of the enemy." He hid in an "old coach every night, with faithful old Sam as his guard" while the rest of her family took refuge in a plantation overseer's "tiny dwelling." She reported:

> *No sooner had we committed our dear father to his solitary confinement on the night I last wrote you, and were endeavouring to console ourselves with the idea that the miserable little hovel we were in was too solitary a situation for us to fear any danger; then while enjoying our frugal supper of Bonny Clabber, honey, etc., a terrible clatter of horses at the door set us all scampering. The British! Nothing but the word British did we hear; upon opening the door, however, we soon discovered a parcel of miserable militia belonging to the neighbourhood. They had called to give notice that the enemy were actually proceeding on their way through the country, but not one of them could say which route they had taken. A consultation of our party was then held, and if we had had one particle of our natural reason*

about us, we should have quietly stayed where we were, but flight had so long been the word that it was determined unanimously that we should lie off in a moment. The nearer the mountains the greater the safety, was the conclusion; so on we traveled through byways and brambles until we could get to the main road leading to Charlottesville. Our design was first to reach a plantation in the neighbourhood of the Springs, where we were at least sure of house room and a bed (a friend of ours having removed his furniture to this place for security); and to this place we proceeded, where we arrived just as the sun appeared in all his glory. With difficulty we got admittance, no soul being in the house, and were just spreading pallets to rest our weary heads, when the landlord, out of breath, reached the house, saying that Tarleton and all his men had just passed, and would catch the Governor before he could reach Charlottesville.

What a panic for us all! Our best beloved father had pursued the same route only a half hour before, Charlottesville being the place appointed for public officers to repair to. Fortunately, however, the enemy had got ahead of him by another road, which he by good luck hearing, he immediately joined us and hurried us back to the selfsame spot [near Louisa Court House] *we had left the night before.*[162]

The dragoons moved into Albemarle County before dawn on the fourth, and by way of a local lane, they reached the main north–south road from Orange Court House to Milton, entering it just north of Mechunk Creek before turning south. Moving "with all the secrecy and celerity possible," according to James Madison, in this neighborhood of large farms at the foot of the Southwest Mountains, Tarleton's men approached several houses looking for sleeping legislators to apprehend before any warning could spread to Charlottesville. One of these plantations was Belvoir, the home of Colonel John Walker, a boyhood friend of Jefferson's who had previously served as an aide on General Washington's staff and in the Continental Congress. Here, the British captured Walker's son-in-law, Francis Kinloch, a South Carolina congressman and coincidently a cousin of one of Tarleton's officers, Captain David Kinloch. Also made prisoner at Belvoir were the brothers of General Nelson, William and Robert Nelson, but Amherst County delegate Ambrose Rucker managed to escape on horseback from Tarleton's dragoons.[163]

North of Belvoir, Tarleton rode with most of his troops to Castle Hill, the plantation of Dr. Thomas Walker, whose son owned Belvoir. The sixty-six-year-old Dr. Walker was a famous physician, Virginia burgess, French and

Frontiersman Daniel Boone was captured by Tarleton's men in Charlottesville. *Library of Congress.*

Indian War officer, early explorer of Kentucky, Indian treaty diplomat, horticulturist, planter and in-law of George Washington.[164] Tarleton later recalled his arrival in "the neighborhood of Doctor Walker's," where "soon after daybreak some of the principal gentlemen of Virginia, who had fled to the borders of the mountains for security, were taken out of their beds: Part were paroled, and left with their families, while others, who were suspected to be more hostile in their sentiments, were carried off."[165] Those staying at Castle Hill were completely surprised by the cavalry's arrival. "We [had] indulged the thought of being far from the enemy, and the pleasure of a good night's repose," wrote one of Walker's guests. Dr. Walker was captured and paroled, along with several others at Castle Hill, including militia Colonel John Syme, Judge Peter Lyons of Hanover County and Delegate Newman Brockenbrough of Essex County. Lyons reported that "as to civility, we all received much more of it than we expected."[166]

"After a halt of half an hour to refresh the horses," Tarleton "moved on toward Charlottesville," via the Louisa Road to the Three Notched Road near Shadwell. Hoping to surprise the governor and assembly, he "approached the Rivanna [River]…with all possible expedition," but his dragoons found that the crossing of the river at Secretary's Ford below Pantops Mountain was blocked by Patriot militiamen led by Captain John Martin. Tarleton's troopers charged across the river and routed the rebels in a furious attack. Writing in the third person, Tarleton reported that "as soon as one hundred cavalry had passed the water, Lieutenant-colonel Tarleton directed them to charge into the town, to continue the confusion of the Americans, and to apprehend, if possible, the governor and assembly."[167]

Jouett's timely warning and the earlier adjournment of the assembly prevented Tarleton from bagging all the legislators, but several of them did not escape. Former lieutenant governor Dudley Diggs and public printer James Hayes were among the prisoners. A delegate clad in buckskin named Daniel Boone from far-off Fayette County (in what is now Kentucky) dallied too long around the courthouse in town loading public records into wagons and failed to evade the dragoons and fusiliers as he began his trek to Staunton. When British troopers heard him referred to as "captain" by a fellow Patriot (possibly Jack Jouett) just outside town, he was marched to Tarleton's headquarters at the Farm, the plantation home of Nicholas Lewis built in 1770, less than one half mile west of the Rivanna River. Lewis was Dr. Walker's son-in-law and the sheriff of Albemarle County but was away serving as an officer in the Continental Army. Using the kitchen building—a small brick structure still standing and largely intact—as his headquarters, Tarleton had Boone held overnight in a nearby coal shed to prevent his escape.[168] Tarleton wrote that the gentlemen prisoners his troopers captured were "treated with kindness and liberality," but "the lower class were secured as prisoners of war" and taken to Cornwallis's headquarters along the James River.[169] Significantly, "the last remaining [printing] press in this Country [was] taken by the Enemy as it was sent out of Town but a few hours before the light Horse entered," Richard Henry Lee reported from his Northern Neck home. "I reckon the want of a press here a most essential injury to our Cause & Country,…the People being now destitute of information and left a prey to Tory lies and bad influences."[170]

The British destroyed what stores they found in the town. Tarleton stated that his troopers and the fusiliers burned one thousand muskets made at Fredericksburg, over 400 barrels of flour, some tobacco and Continental uniforms.[171] The dragoons, however, missed destroying 256 barrels of gunpowder stored in a warehouse near Milton when they approached Charlottesville by Secretary's Ford. Lafayette later minimized the extent of the losses in Charlottesville due to the raid. He reported the "trifling" damages as 150 stands of arms, some gunpowder and county court records, and another Virginian described the loss as "not great."[172] One Virginia gentleman also deplored the conduct of the delegates, too, saying that many "returned home dispersing the news of our misfortune & their disgrace without expressing a thought about any future collection of the Legislature."[173]

Enniscorthy is where Jefferson initially fled to avoid Tarleton's Raid. The current house in image is from the nineteenth century. *Author photograph.*

While Tarleton's cavalry swarmed into Charlottesville, the scene above the town at Jefferson's home was also dramatic. After Captain Jouett warned the governor of the enemy's imminent approach, Jefferson sat down to a leisurely breakfast with his guests. He soon arranged for his family to leave the imperiled mountaintop, accompanied by William Short, one of his young protégés and a law student at the College of William and Mary. Short escorted Martha Jefferson and her two children by carriage to Enniscorthy, John Coles II's plantation in southern Albemarle County, situated about fourteen miles to the south on Green Mountain.[174]

As Jefferson later recalled, "the Speakers, with their Colleagues, returned to Charlottesville" after their morning meal, packed up what belongings they could "and with the other members of the legislature, had barely time to get out of the way." The governor, however, did not act in haste. He ordered his horse shod at his nearby Shadwell farm across the Rivanna River and then brought to Monticello.[175] Captain Christopher Hudson, a young Virginia military officer, soon arrived on Jefferson's little mountain to warn the governor again of the approach of a party of British Legion cavalrymen. "I was convinced the situation was truly critical," Hudson later recalled, but he found Jefferson "perfectly tranquil, and undisturbed." Within ten minutes, the British were coming up the mountain, and Jefferson finally decided to ride south over nearby Carter's Mountain to avoid capture. "At my earnest request he left his house," Hudson wrote.[176]

At some point after his family had departed, Jefferson climbed Carter's Mountain, carrying a sword cane and a collapsible telescope. From this high perch, he could see into Charlottesville. According to tradition, Jefferson first spied no enemy troops in the town using his telescope and began to walk down the mountain. Realizing he had dropped his cane at the crown of the ridge, he returned to retrieve it, at which point he looked again at Charlottesville with his powerful glass. This time he observed British dragoons in the streets far below, and consequently hurried down the rise to mount his stallion Caractacus and flee his home.[177] Jefferson later wrote that "knowing that in the public road I should be liable to fall in with the enemy, I went thro' the woods."[178] He escaped along obscure forest paths and farm lanes and then likely rode on the east side of Carter's Mountain rather than the more heavily traveled Scottsville Road, on the west slope. The careworn governor, according to his friend James Madison, had a "very narrow escape."[179]

The dragoons Tarleton sent to capture Jefferson at Monticello made up a small detachment under Captain Kenneth McLeod. The cavalrymen approached the lofty residence by way of Secretary's Ford, perhaps with a slave or Loyalist guide. No doubt Jefferson was anxious for the fate of his home and valuable possessions within it as he fled the mountaintop, but he need not have worried. "Captain McLeod preserved every thing with sacred care, during about eighteen hours he remained there," Jefferson later wrote with relief and reported a few years after the war that Tarleton had specifically ordered "to suffer nothing to be injured" in the house.[180] McLeod does not seem to have ordered a pursuit of Jefferson, whose whereabouts the British officer was unable to ascertain from the plantation's slaves.[181]

A tradition in Jefferson's family and among descendants of the Hemingses, an enslaved family who labored at Monticello and were closely related to Martha Jefferson, holds that Martin Hemings and Caesar, both slaves, were hiding the estate's valuable silver plate under the plank floor of one of the house's porticos just as the enemy troopers arrived. Hemings quickly slammed down the boards, trapping Caesar in the small space beneath the porch, where he remained for eighteen hours during the British visit to the plantation.[182] Family legend also held that McLeod was shown through the house by Hemings and stopped to admire Jefferson's impressive study, its books and curiosities. The officer locked the door, gave Hemings the key "and bade him refer any of his soldiers inquiring for it to himself."[183]

Geddes, home of Colonel Huge Rose in northern Amherst County, is where Jefferson and his family stayed briefly after leaving Monticello. *Octavia Starbuck photograph.*

Once united with his family at Enniscorthy, Jefferson decided to move farther from the enemy to the Amherst County home of Colonel Hugh Rose, forty miles to the southwest. The family went first to Joplin's Ordinary at a ford on the Rockfish River, about a dozen miles upstream from the James River. They stayed nearby overnight, crossed the river with help from local slaves the next day and passed through Findlay's Gap, fourteen miles south. Eventually, Jefferson and his party reached Hughes's plantation, called Geddes, close to the Tye River. The plantation included a story-and-a-half frame house built in 1762 on high ground at the foot of the Blue Ridge Mountains. Hughes was a member of the House of Delegates, a militia officer and a friend of Jefferson. While his family rested at Geddes after their tiring journey, Jefferson hurried back to Monticello on horseback to assess the plantation's condition. Relieved that so little had been disturbed there, he returned to his family at Rose's home and soon set out for his Poplar Forest retreat in Bedford County, west of Lynchburg, where he would remain until late July.[184]

Meanwhile, as Tarleton and his command trotted west to strike Charlottesville, early on June 2, Colonel Simcoe began his rapid advance from Cook's Ford against the Continental stores at Point of Fork, at the confluence of the Rivanna and James Rivers. He described his preparations in camp:

Lord Cornwallis informed him, that Steuben's force consisted of three or four hundred men; and as the Queen's Rangers were so debilitated by the fatigues of the climate, etc., as to have scarcely more than two hundred infantry and one hundred cavalry, fit for duty, his Lordship ordered the 71st regiment, under Captain Hutchinson, consisting of two hundred rank and file, to join him: at Lieutenant Colonel Simcoe's request, a three pounder [cannon] was annexed. The incessant marches of the Rangers, and their distance from their stores, had so worn out their shoes, that, on Lt. Colonel Simcoe's calling for a return, it appeared that nearly fifty men were absolutely barefooted; upon assembling them, when they were informed that they were wanted for active employment, and that those who chose to stay with the army might do so, there was not a man who would remain behind the corps.[185]

Simcoe's column included an advance party of "twenty huzzars…mounted on the fleetest horses," followed by "the light infantry company and the Hessian riflemen."[186]

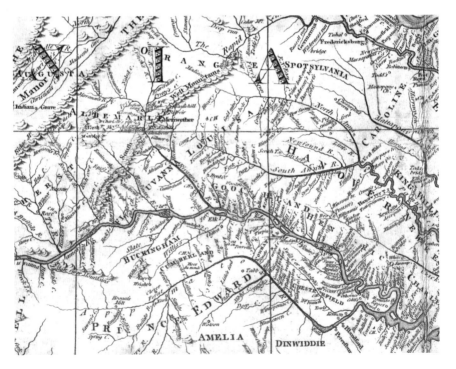

Period map detail showing Monticello, Point of Fork, Elk-hill and other sites reached by British troops west of Goochland Court House. *Library of Congress.*

Simcoe's troops crossed the South Anna River at Ground Squirrel Bridge and then rode west to Byrd's Ordinary, a well-known travelers' rest in western Louisa County along the Three Chopt Road. From here, the British went south to Napier's Ford on the Rivanna River, near the original Fluvanna County Court House and the mouth of Ballinger Creek. During the British progression, "not a person escaped…and the advance cavalry were so managed as to totally conceal the advance of the infantry," Simcoe recalled. At Napier's Ford, Simcoe's men learned from captured militiamen that Baron von Steuben was at Point of Fork, had removed most of the military stores to the south side of the James River and was "superintending the transportation of the remainder with the greatest dispatch." Simcoe "determined to march, with the utmost celerity, towards Baron von Steuben, hoping to cut off his rear guard," still north of the river. Simcoe's troops crossed to the west side of the Rivanna, got within two miles of Point of Fork and captured a patrol of American dragoons led by a French officer.[187] Some of Simcoe's Huzzars switched clothes with the American captives so that he could send them to the American depot to capture von Steuben there, with support from British cavalry, infantry and the one artillery piece with the force. By the time Simcoe's men arrived at the Fork on June 5, however, they saw von Steuben's troops on the south side of the James, as the baron had been warned of the British approach the previous day by Major Richard Call of the Continental Dragoons.[188] With few boats available to the British to make a crossing, it appeared that attacking the Americans was impossible.[189]

Undaunted, Simcoe decided on a ruse in order to make his force appear larger and dupe the rebels into fleeing their position on the far riverbank. "Every effort was now made to persuade the enemy that the party was Earl Cornwallis's army," he wrote, "that they might leave the opposite shore, which was covered with arms and stores." Simcoe ordered the commander of the Seventy-first Regiment "clothed in red" to "advance as near to the banks of the [James] as he could with perfect safety, and without the hazard of a single man, from the enemy's shot, who had lined the opposite shore." He also halted his baggage and numerous camp followers on the summit of the hill to his rear, "and in that position [they] made the appearance of a numerous corps." The rest of the troops were placed on the neck of the fork, their strength concealed by the woods. He ordered the cannon to fire once from the north bank at von Steuben's position, a well-aimed shot that killed an officer's horse.[190]

That night Simcoe was "apprehensive" that von Steuben would attack him with his Continentals and militia troops by crossing the river higher

Point of Fork was the location of the Patriot forces' arsenal and depot. The James River is on the left, and the Rivanna River is on the right. Von Steuben retreated from Simcoe's advance to the south bank, on the left side of photograph. *Author photograph.*

up and trapping him between the Rivanna and the James, a difficult spot from which to retreat. Simcoe wrote that he "would have quitted his camp had he not thought the troops too much fatigued, to search for a more favorable position."[191]

The British cavalryman need not have worried. During the night, the British could hear the rebels destroying their boats and saw them "making up their fires," in preparation of leaving their position. Two American deserters sneaked across the river in a canoe after dark and reported that von Steuben had left his camp and headed south to Cumberland Court House, about twenty miles away (the baron actually retreated about six miles downstream toward the mouth of the Willis River near Carter's Ferry). "When daylight appeared, there was not an enemy to be seen," Simcoe wrote, and the south side of the river was found to be "covered with the enemy's stores," including cannons and mortars. "He must have believed that the whole of Earl Cornwallis's army were in pursuit of him, or he would have scarcely abandoned such a quantity of stores," Simcoe gloated. A small British light infantry detachment was sent across the James in canoes to destroy the supplies and equipment not needed for Simcoe's troops, which took most of the day. "A guard of twenty or thirty men would have effectually prevented the Rangers from destroying" the stores, Simcoe surmised.[192] His men also destroyed most of the property and buildings at the arsenal situated along the Rivanna River, although David Ross, owner of the Point of Fork land and a commercial agent for Virginia, wrote that the local inhabitants "stole as much or more than the British destroyed."[193]

Simcoe left Point of Fork on June 7, having wrecked—according to his report—2,500 mostly unserviceable stands of arms, "a large quantity of gunpowder, case shot, etc., several casks of saltpetre, sulpher, and brimstone, and upwards of sixty hogsheads of rum and brandy, several chests of carpenters' tools, and upwards of four hundred entrenching tools, with casks of flints, sail cloth and wagons." Also captured and thrown in the river were a thirteen-inch mortar, five brass eighteen-inch howitzers and "four long brass nine pounders," all French-made pieces "in excellent order."[194] Von Steuben later reported insignificant losses at the arsenal, but the damages were clearly real. Simcoe had "executed the plan committed to his direction with great zeal and indefatigable attention," Tarleton concluded.[195]

When Lord Cornwallis sent Tarleton and Simcoe on their swift mounted raids to destroy supplies and capture provincial legislators, he did not intend to remain idle at Cook's Ford. Rather, his main army would follow in Simcoe's path for some distance through Goochland County by way of the River Road along the north side of the James.[196] The British general planned to unite with his two cavalry commanders near Point of Fork and to continue the destruction of enemy supply caches south of Charlottesville. No longer chasing Lafayette or intending to devastate Fredericksburg, the British army turned west to proceed with what General Washington later termed "rapid and devious movements."[197]

Before dawn on June 3, the British force left its camps and marched west below the North Anna River for several miles. The following day, the troops turned south at Brown's Ordinary and passed "Scotchtown" on their way to the Ground Squirrel Bridge, where they crossed the South Anna River. Once across, Cornwallis halted his men on the fourth south of the river in Hanover County along a winding country road, on which were several extensive plantations. The general and his officers made their headquarters at "Mount Brilliant," a brick house west of Stone Horse Creek, once owned by the father of Patrick Henry. The house had recently been the residence of a Virginia high court justice, Robert Carter Nicholas Sr., until his death the previous year. His widow, Anne Cary Nicholas, was residing in the house with her children when the neighborhood was invaded by the redcoats, who that night were given an extra rum ration in honor of King George III's birthday.

Mount Brilliant, the Nicholas home in Hanover County, is where the British army camped in early June. *Author photograph.*

No doubt fueled by liquor, the troops heavily damaged the plantation and those around it, confiscating or destroying livestock, orchards, fences, barns, hay and valuables. Additionally, the large number of runaway slaves who accompanied the British force on the campaign in central Virginia also consumed a massive amount of provisions from the area's farms.[198]

A Virginian described the scene of the Nicholas estate after the British marched away the next day:

> *The day after the Enemy left Mrs. Nicholas's I went over to her home where I saw the devastation caused by the Enemy encamping there, for they encamped in her plantation all around the house. The fences [were] pulled down & much of them burnt; Many cattle, hogs, sheep and poultry of all sorts killed; 150 barrels of corn eat up or wasted; and the offal of the cattle, etc., with dead horses and pieces of flesh all in a putrefying state scattered over the plantation.*[199]

Cornwallis's redcoats, Hessians, provincials, artillerymen and camp followers, along with the army's guns and wagons, left Mount Brilliant on June 5 and proceeded about twelve miles south to Napier's Mill, situated on Horsepen Creek in eastern Goochland County. Halting briefly for rest and water at the mill, the column advanced southwest on the Glebe Road to Belmont, a five-hundred-acre farm owned by Thomas Fleming Bates, located at the end of the Glebe Road along Cheneys Creek, a few miles west of Goochland Court House.[200]

Having marched about twenty miles that day, Cornwallis's soldiers and hangers-on encamped at the Bates plantation and destroyed or consumed much of what they found there. After the war, Bates made a claim for losses greater than any other resident of Goochland. Corn, oats, fencing, barrels, tools, "well blooded mares," a colt, four "valuable oxen," a "fine English bull" and milk cows were all lost to him during the unwelcome visit from the enemy's troops. And like many other Patriot Virginia planters that spring and summer, Bates lost slaves. His 1782 petition to the Virginia legislature included claims for a "valuable Negro fellow, 30 yrs old" worth £100 and a "likely girl 14 years old" worth the same amount.[201]

Bates's claim is a reminder that many of Virginia's slaves took the opportunity of the British invasion of Virginia to escape their masters and plantation homes. One Virginia observer wrote that freedom-seeking slaves "flocked to the enemy from all quarters, even from very remote parts" and that "some plantations were entirely cleared, & not a single Negro remained." He also noted that the British "enticed and flattered" slaves to join their column "whenever they had an opportunity." Richard Henry Lee of Westmoreland County wrote that it was "the case of all those who were near the enemy" that the slaves went off with the British, adding that Cornwallis had "been traversing an undefended part of Virginia, with an army employed in taking off Negroes[,] plate &c & destroying Corn, Cattle, & Tob[acc]o." Lee also reported that some Virginians had "lost every slave they had in the world" and that "force, fraud, intrigue, [and] theft" were used by the British "to delude these unhappy people and defraud their masters!" In August 1781, Lord Cornwallis wrote that "great numbers have come to us from different parts of the country" but denied that slaves were taken by his orders.[202]

Since the American Revolution, the number of blacks who escaped bondage by following the invading British army in the 1781 campaign has been a matter of debate among historians and Virginians (who were seeking compensation for runaway slaves and trying to avoid paying prewar debts to British creditors per the 1783 Treaty of Paris).[203] One recent historian has written that "30,000 freedom-loving blacks…joined Cornwallis in the summer of 1781" and states that "by the middle of June 1781, at least 12,000 runaway slaves were with Cornwallis' army." He also quotes Jefferson's claim that Virginia lost "30,000 slaves" in 1781 during Cornwallis's invasion.[204]

Recent research has cast convincing doubt on these numbers, and period accounts show that they have been significantly exaggerated. For instance, a Hessian officer with Cornwallis's army noted that there were about 4,000 runaway slaves with the British in central Virginia in June, and other sources suggest a lower figure—perhaps 2,000 with Cornwallis and another 1,500 at Portsmouth that summer. Jefferson's number of 30,000 is a significant overstatement based on little empirical support. The modern suggestion of 12,000 enslaved Virginians—to say nothing of the "30,000 slaves"—accompanying Cornwallis's soldiers as they marched through a rural region of plantations, small farms and large swathes of sparsely inhabited wooded terrain is inconsistent with the enormous logistical burden this would have placed on the British army providing the runaways with even meager provisions. Even though the liberated slaves foraged from local plantations on the march, it is doubtful that the region's farms could have sustained such a large host as inflated claims have declared. Given that Norfolk, Virginia's largest city, had a population of 6,000 in 1775, it is implausible that 30,000 runaway noncombatants could have been supported in the British army's wake while on the move in a rural district. Equally telling is the fact that no British officer reported anything like such a large number of slave followers with Cornwallis, and his lordship makes very few references to these camp followers in his letters of the time. "No Negroes have been taken by the British troops by my orders nor to my knowledge," he wrote in August, and his report that "great numbers have come to us" does not indicate he meant tens of thousands of runaways.[205]

Notwithstanding these overstated numbers, Virginians were impacted by the loss of those slaves who freed themselves, many of whom acted as guides for British forces in the state, pilots for Royal Navy ships and worked for Cornwallis's army as laborers, cooks, laundresses, drivers, drovers and servants. Lafayette complained that the British learned where to confiscate horses in order to get "a formidable cavalry" by what he called a "treaty of alliance with the negroes" as they approached plantations on their destructive march. Moreover, the added number of people who attached themselves to Cornwallis's forces added to the destruction of Virginia farms and plantations in his column's path. "Any place this horde approached," wrote one of Cornwallis's Hessian officers, "was eaten clean, like an acre invaded by a swarm of locusts."[206] In August, for instance, a British detachment of eight hundred cavalrymen "and 600 negroes" from Portsmouth ravaged a York County plantation, where they burned fences, "spoiled 23,000 corn-hills, [and] carried away

4,000 bundles of good old fodder." Most of these runaway slaves met a cruel fate by the time Cornwallis surrendered his army to Washington at Yorktown in October 1781, dying of disease and exposure and largely cast off by the British forces they had initially regarded as their liberators.[207]

From the ransacked Bates property, Cornwallis sent a brief message on June 5 to Tarleton, then operating between Point of Fork and Charlottesville. "I can subsist a few days between Goochland Court House and the Fork," the general wrote, "if you can strike a blow without risque to your corps, do it." Perhaps the earl recalled Tarleton's impetuous attack at Cowpens five months earlier when cautioning him with this note.[208]

The British commander soon led his invaders a dozen miles west along the River Road on June 7 and reached Elk-hill Plantation, a Goochland farm of several hundred acres along the James River about three miles east of Point of Fork. This land had been purchased in 1778 by Thomas and Martha Jefferson from her half sister, Anne Wayles Skipwith, who had inherited it from her father, John Wayles.[209] On the property was a frame house that General Cornwallis used as his headquarters. Jefferson described it as "a good dwelling house, of 4 rooms below, & two above, with convenient outhouses, on a high and beautiful position, commanding a fine view of the Blue mountains, of James river for several miles, & of Elk-island," to the south. This structure, built before 1760, is no longer standing and was situated to the northwest of the nearby nineteenth-century house called Elk-hill.[210]

Elk-hill, Jefferson's Goochland farm, is where Cornwallis's troops encamped for several days. *Author photograph.*

Although British dragoons had left Monticello largely undamaged, this was not the case at Jefferson's Elk-hill property. He described his losses in detail:

> *Lord Cornwallis…proceeded to the point of fork, and encamped his army from thence all along the main James river to a seat of mine called Elk-hill, opposite to Elk island and a little below the mouth of the Byrd creek. He remained in this position ten days, his own head quarters being in my house at that place. I had had time to remove most of the effects out of the house. He destroyed all my growing crops of corn and tobacco, he burned all my barns containing the same articles of the last year, having first taken what corn he wanted, he used, as was to be expected, all my stocks of cattle, sheep, and hogs for the sustenance of his army, and carried off all the horses capable of service: of those too young for service he cut the throats, and he burnt all the fences on the plantation, so as to leave it an absolute waste. He carried off also about 30. slaves: had this been to give them freedom he would have done right, but it was to consign them to inevitable death from the small pox and putrid fever then raging in his camp. This I knew afterwards to have been the fate of 27. of them. I never had news of the remaining three, but presume they shared the same fate. When I say that Lord Cornwallis did all this, I do not mean that he carried about the torch in his own hands, but that it was all done under his eye, the situation of the house, in which he was, commanding a view of every part of the plantation, so that he must have seen every fire. I relate these things on my own knowledge in a great degree, as I was on the ground soon after he left it.[211]*

Jefferson claimed damages of over £1,500 suffered at this plantation.[212] Cornwallis "treated the rest of the neighborhood in much the same style" as he had Elk-hill, but Jefferson thought "not with that spirit of total extermination with which he seemed to rage over my possessions." The governor later called his losses a "useless and barbarous injury," although he certainly was not the only planter in Virginia's Piedmont or Tidewater regions to suffer at the hands of the enemy's marauders.[213]

British cavalry units conducted several raids on nearby plantations along the James River between Elk-hill and Goochland Court House. Cornwallis also attempted to destroy additional rebel magazines nearby, particularly since the mounted detachments under Simcoe and Tarleton had rejoined his army. On June 9, he sent Simcoe west with a mounted detachment of the Queen's Rangers to Seven Islands, located in the James River just below the mouth of the Hardware River. There, the British "destroyed one hundred and fifty barrels of gunpowder, and burnt all of the tobacco in the warehouses on the river side, returning with some rebel militia whom he had surprised and made prisoners."[214]

On the same day, Cornwallis ordered Tarleton to leave Elk-hill before dawn on the tenth with his cavalry and mounted infantry to "destroy any stores you may find" at Old Albemarle Court House, situated on a ridge near Scott's Ferry on the James River twenty miles south of Charlottesville. This location on a large northward bend of the James included the former courthouse building from the 1740s, a small prison and a few additional structures, all used to house supplies above the river's flood plain southwest of the ferry landing on a plantation called Valmont. He was authorized to "strike a blow at Baron Steuben" if the enemy was still positioned on the south bank of the James and to "defeat and disperse" Virginia's newly raised Continental forces under his command. Cornwallis also urged Tarleton, if he "should see a probability of success," to push his troops south

> *to destroy all the enemy's stores and tobacco between James river and the Dan; and if there should be a quantity of provisions or corn collected at a private house, I would have you destroy it, even although there should be no proof of its being intended for public service, leaving enough for the support of the family; as there is the greatest reason to apprehend that such provisions will be ultimately appropriated by the enemy to the use of General Green's army, which, from the present state of the Carolinas, must depend on this province for its supplies.*

Tarleton was to attach soldiers from the Seventy-sixth Regiment to his legion for this expedition, but before he set out from Jefferson's plantation, Cornwallis received intelligence that the stores at the old courthouse had been removed and that von Steuben was no longer nearby. "The expedition, therefore, was countermanded," Tarleton reported.[215]

What Tarleton left unsaid regarding the canceled raid is that Cornwallis had become cautious upon receiving word of Lafayette's approach from the north. Cornwallis sent out cavalry patrols to scout the rebel force, and by June 13, Tarleton knew that part of Lafayette's soldiers were close by. Any further attempts to destroy more enemy supply caches around Charlottesville would now be perilous. Having been at Elk-hill for several days, Cornwallis knew he was far from the British base at Portsmouth, and even the nearest convenient place of resupply on the James River near Richmond was over fifty miles from western Goochland. Based on these considerations, the British commander prudently began to make preparations to retire east.[216]

"VIRGINIA IS NOT CONQUERED"

Wary Opponents Along the James

Those generals who have had but little experience attempt to protect every point, while those who are better acquainted with their profession, having only the capital object in view, guard against a decisive blow, and acquiesce in small misfortunes to avoid greater.
—*Frederick the Great, mid-eighteenth century*

As the three British columns advanced west from Hanover, Lafayette kept on the march to link his troops with General Wayne's long-delayed brigade of Pennsylvanians. The enemy's dragoons and light troops still prevented the marquis from gaining accurate intelligence of British movements so that the marquis was not yet aware that Cornwallis had turned his attention toward Point of Fork, Charlottesville and Old Albemarle Court House. Still assuming that the primary targets of the redcoats' operations were Fredericksburg and his own troops, Lafayette moved north across the Rapidan River, which put a significant barrier between his soldiers and the British. As one Culpeper County militia draftee recalled decades later, "We were pursued by Cornwallis's army and being overpowered it was thought more advisable to retreat than to go into an unequal combat."[217]

A number of period sources and modern histories of the campaign state that Lafayette's troops crossed the Rapidan River at Germanna Ford, located five miles northwest of the Wilderness Run bivouac site. This route not only would have allowed the Patriot forces to use a well-known crossing of the Rapidan but also would have been a direct way for Lafayette to move closer to Wayne's approaching regiments. A French map produced shortly after the war shows Lafayette's command fording the river near Germanna, a former settlement of German ironworkers and miners originating in the early 1700s.[218] A Virginia historical marker recently erected near the site of the Wilderness Run Bridge states that while Lafayette reconnoitered at Ely's Ford downriver, his Continentals and militiamen waded the Rapidan at Germanna Ford.[219]

What exists of Lafayette's 1781 correspondence does not report any crossing of the Rapidan at Germanna Ford. In fact, on June 4, he wrote to Wayne from Ely's Ford, which was northeast of Wilderness Run, although he does not specifically state that his army would cross there. Many historical maps of the nineteenth and twentieth centuries depict the marquis's line of march by way of Ely's Ford, and the location of his army's next encampment in Culpeper County might also support this thesis.[220] Additionally, an often overlooked letter written from the Wilderness Run encampment on June 4 from William Constable, an aide to Lafayette, to Captain Thomas Drew of the Virginia troops states, "We will cross at Ely's Ford today to join Wayne."[221]

Ely's Ford is where Lafayette's army crossed the Rapidan River west of Fredericksburg. *Author photograph.*

Although the available evidence is not conclusive, it would appear from the contemporary letters of Lafayette and Constable that the army did in fact splash across the Rapidan at Ely's Ford, not Germanna Ford.

Once across the river, the American troops turned west and, on the afternoon of June 4, halted at what Lafayette called "Culpeper Church."[222] This was the Anglican house of worship in eastern Culpeper County properly known as the Lower or Great Fork Church, due to its location within the fork of the Rapidan and Rappahannock Rivers. Built near the site of an earlier chapel, the frame church around which Lafayette's men rested was built in 1733, but it is no longer standing today.[223] Of note, the colonial road the church once stood on was then part of Ely's Ford Road, giving further credence to the conclusion that Lafayette crossed the Rapidan at that ford. Lafayette wrote to Wayne from the Great Fork Church on June 5, directing him to bring his Continentals to Raccoon Ford, located on the Rapidan River about seven or eight miles west of the marquis' position, so the two forces could finally combine.[224]

By June 6, Lafayette's troops had reached Raccoon Ford, ten miles south of Culpeper. "The movements of the enemy render it of the highest importance," he wrote to Wayne, then located about thirty miles to the northeast, "that we may soon come near to them...I think a junction with you must be our first object." He also suggested that Wayne should meet him in advance of his troops that evening, but inclement weather may have delayed a meeting.[225]

Lafayette's soldiers were able to rest at Raccoon Ford until the eighth, when they resumed marching south through the hills of Orange County. The marquis soon halted his army near modern Rhoadesville, about seven miles east of Orange Court House, on the night of June 8–9.[226] By June 10, Lafayette was at Brock's Bridge on the North Anna River, ahead of his marching column, reconnoitering his intended path toward Charlottesville. The welcome news must have reached him later in the day that several miles to the rear, Wayne's brigade had finally caught up with the marquis' detachment south of Raccoon Ford.[227]

The story of Brigadier General Anthony Wayne's troops marching to join Lafayette in Virginia began five months earlier in the Pennsylvanians' winter camps in northern New Jersey. In order to move Wayne's men from the Continental Army's Northern Department to the southern theater of operations, Washington and Wayne had to overcome an insurrection among the soldiers, logistical shortfalls, the contentious issue of back pay and, finally, a march of over 150 miles.

Above: Raccoon Ford on the Rapidan was crossed by the forces of Generals Lafayette and Wayne in June before their soldiers united in Orange County. *Author photograph.*

Left: Brigadier General Anthony Wayne. *Library of Congress.*

In early January 1781, Washington received a startling letter from Wayne with news of alarming events at Morristown, New Jersey. At the frigid camps of the Pennsylvania line, "the most general and unhappy mutiny suddenly took place" on the night of January 1. A Pennsylvania officer was killed in the mayhem and another severely wounded. Half of the angry troops were marching to confront Congress at Princeton, New Jersey, where it was then in session. Wayne had moved some trustworthy Continental dragoons to intercept the malcontents before they reached Princeton, but "what their temper may be I can not tell." Perhaps Washington was somewhat relieved to learn that the mutineers did not desert to the enemy at New York but that "their General cry is to be Discharged." Still, this was a dangerous situation, not just because the enemy might exploit the discontent within the Pennsylvanians' ranks but also because these were the troops Washington planned to send south to reinforce General Greene.[228]

The Pennsylvanians were primarily disgruntled over the terms of their enlistments. The previous fall, Congress had reorganized the Continental Army, with changes to go into effect on January 1, 1781. This restructuring of the regiments convinced many of the Pennsylvania soldiers that they were no longer bound by the terms of their original enlistment agreements made in 1777. Coupled with the unrelieved shortages of pay, provisions and proper clothing, hundreds of soldiers rebelled in their icy cantonment. By the end of January, congressional representatives had reached agreements with the soldiers and released over 1,200 men from military service, in addition to making promises to improve the conditions in the camps and issuing back pay. Wayne predicted that many of the released soldiers would eventually rejoin their units. About 1,200 men remained within three reorganized Pennsylvania battalions at the end of the month, soon joined by one company and six guns of the Fourth Continental Artillery.[229]

By March, Washington expected Wayne to proceed to the Southern Department in support of either Lafayette or Greene as circumstances required. Although Wayne had procured new shoes and uniforms for most of the men with whom he intended to march south, the failure of Congress to make up the troops' pay shortages led them to refuse to leave their camps. "I have been knocking at every door from the [state] Council up to Congress to little purpose," reported Wayne, but "they all present me that Gorgon head—an empty treasury." Some in Congress worried that if money were lent to Pennsylvania to satisfy its troops, the soldiers from other states would be encouraged to mutiny as well.[230] The efforts to resolve this frustrating impasse took months. Washington wrote to Wayne

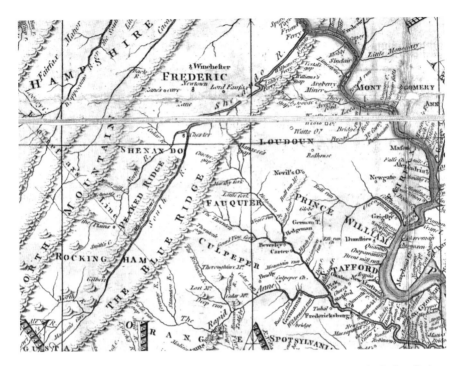

Colonial-era map showing locations along Wayne's route to join Lafayette, including Red House, Neavil's Mill, Germantown and Elk Run Church. *Library of Congress.*

and Major General Arthur St. Clair, commander of the Pennsylvania Line, imploring them to get their troops "collected and forwarded as early as possible to succor the States which are now the Theatre of War, and reinforce the Southern Army."[231]

Finally, on May 26, Wayne was able to move about one thousand men to York, Pennsylvania, although another mutiny broke out before they marched. This incident of unrest was quickly and forcefully put down, and seven of its leaders were promptly executed in front of their comrades.[232] From York, the troops proceeded through Frederick, Maryland, to the Potomac River, which they crossed into Virginia "in bad boats" at Noland's Ferry near Leesburg on May 31.[233] One of the boats sank during the crossings, with the loss of "some ammunition and a few men drowned." On that day, Wayne wrote to the marquis (then at Davenport's Ford) that his brigade and cannons would be over the Potomac by the next morning, "when we shall move as light as possible by divesting ourselves of all the heavy baggage." On the following day, he again wrote to Lafayette, reporting that his soldiers were headed south, "which is performing a march of thirty miles in two days, besides

Site of Noland's Ferry on the Potomac River northeast of Leesburg, where General Wayne's men crossed into Virginia. *Richard C. Maass II photograph.*

passing the troops[,] artillery & baggage over the Potowmack, in four little boats." Still Wayne assured the marquis that "every fatigue and difficulty is surmounted by our anxiety for the wished junction" of the troops.[234]

After marching on the Carolina Road through the "very small town" of Leesburg on June 3,[235] Wayne's troops and their wagons crossed Goose Creek at Cox's Mill and camped nearby in the rain. According to a Pennsylvania officer, here "the houses represent indolence and poverty," and he saw firsthand "the wretchedness of slavery." Leaving the heavy baggage and the sick soldiers at Cox's Mill on June 4, Wayne's men "marched through a low country, road being very bad" to "the Red house," a large brick ordinary at the junction of Thoroughfare Gap Road and the Carolina Road, where they camped north of Broad Run in western Prince William County. One officer recalled that the men were "seldom allowed to eat until twelve o'clock, when the arms were stacked, knapsacks taken off, and water sent for by parties." Wayne advised Lafayette that day that he would continue his march to Orange Court House in continuing rain.[236]

The following day the troops marched twelve miles to the hamlet of Greenwich in Prince William County. Farther south, the column turned west onto the Dumfries Road and then went south again into Fauquier County,

Above: The site of Neavil's Ordinary and mill at today's Auburn, in Fauquier County. *Author photograph.*

Left: Original section of Rougue's Road near Germantown in Fauquier County. *Author photograph.*

crossing Cedar Run at Neavil's Ordinary using a shallow ford by a mill there. From here, the men walked south to Turkey Run, on the banks of which they rested for the night "in the open fields."[237]

South of Turkey Run on June 6, Wayne pushed his men onward "in a very poor country" along Rougue's Road through continual rains to Licking Creek, where the soldiers briefly refreshed themselves at the settlement of Germantown, six miles south of Neavil's Ordinary. Five miles farther to the southeast, the regiments arrived at Elk Run Church on a line of march toward Fredericksburg. This prominent Anglican structure was Fauquier County's first established church, a brick cruciform structure built on a stone foundation in the late 1750s but no longer standing today. Nearby were a tavern and a few small shops. From Elk Run Church, Wayne advised Lafayette that the foul weather had "injured" the men, arms and ammunition, so he would march about nine miles southwest and "halt this side [north] of the Rappahannock on Norman's Ford to refresh & furbish us tomorrow."[238] This projected movement also signified that Fredericksburg was no longer Wayne's goal; instead, he sought to meet Lafayette's troops farther west, in Orange County.

The foundation of Elk Run Church in Fauquier County was revealed by archaeologists in 2006. Wayne's Pennsylvania troops camped here in early June. *Courtesy Elk Run Church Site Preservation Committee.*

Before noon on the seventh, Wayne and his Continentals arrived at Norman's Ford, a wide crossing of the Rappahannock, where he wrote to Lafayette that because of the "deluge of rain which fell last night," the river was then impassable. Some local militiamen were there to build rafts for the crossing, but Wayne complained that they constructed only one, which was too "badly executed" to risk the army's ammunition supply on the high water. He assured Lafayette that "we shall lose nothing by this halt…as our cartridges wanted overhauling and airing and our arms repairing" due to the incessant rains of the last week. He predicted that on the following day, he would reach about halfway between Norman's and Raccoon Fords, probably at York, six miles east of Culpeper. At least part of his men marched twenty-one miles on June 8, through country a Pennsylvania officer described as "very poor and buildings very small," though their exact route is unknown.[239]

After walking south about eight miles from York, Wayne's corps on June 9 waded eighty yards across the muddy Rapidan River at Raccoon Ford, then walked another several miles south before halting for the night on Mountain Run. The troops began their next day's march at 5:00 a.m., headed toward the North Anna River. The long-anticipated union of the Pennsylvanians with Lafayette's hard-marching Continentals occurred on the road south of Raccoon Ford in Orange County. Although he "expected that the junction would take place sooner" and that Wayne's brigade "would be more numerous," the marquis must have been pleased and greatly relieved to receive these Continental reinforcements to add to the 1,800 Virginia militia troops also with his army. One of the Pennsylvania officers wrote that Lafayette's men "look as if they were fit for business. They are chiefly all light infantry, dressed in frocks and over-alls of linen." He could now move south with a respectable force to face the British, who had by then extended their depredations over sixty miles to the west of their Cook's Ford camp.[240]

There is some dispute as to the exact date Wayne's forces met with the marquis' troops marching south of Raccoon Ford. The most recent editor of Lafayette's papers, Stanley J. Idzerda, gives the date as June 10, as do three of Wayne's First Pennsylvania Regiment officers in their journals. However, Captain Benjamin Bartholomew of the Fifth Pennsylvania recorded in his journal that the date was June 11. One of Lafayette's prominent twentieth-century biographers, Louis Gottschalk, also gives the date as the eleventh. Lafayette does not specify a date for the union in his memoirs, and the only known letter he wrote on June 10 places him at Brock's Bridge, well south of Raccoon Ford. Lafayette's known progress toward Charlottesville

The site of Brock's Bridge, where Lafayette's army crossed the North Anna River en route to Boswell's Tavern in Louisa County. *Author photograph.*

and details found in Wayne's correspondence seem to support the earlier date of June 10. As stated earlier, on June 7, Wayne predicted crossing the Rappahannock at Norman's Ford the next day—that is to say, June 8—and anticipated marching about eight or nine miles to a place "about half way between Normans and Raccoon Fords tomorrow evening." This would place his troops at York, and from there, Raccoon Ford was fewer than seven miles farther south. Presumably Wayne's men could march the next day, June 9, to Raccoon Ford on the Rapidan and meet Lafayette's command along the road to Brock's Bridge the following day. This supposition, of course, does not rule out June 11 as the date the two detachments united, but given that all the troops under Lafayette and Wayne reached Mechunk Creek—about forty-five miles from Raccoon Ford—no later than June 12, the date of June 10 for the combination of forces in Orange County seems more probable. It should also be noted that contrary to many later historical works, the troops of the two generals united on the road *south* of Raccoon Ford and not *at* the ford, which Lafayette's correspondence makes clear.[241]

After being joined by Wayne's Continentals, Lafayette moved his reinforced command into Louisa County at Brock's Bridge, a crossing of the North Anna River about ten miles southeast of Orange Court House.[242] From here, the troops advanced to cross the South Anna River at what later became known as Munford's Bridge and then marched another mile to encamp around Boswell's Tavern, where Tarleton had burned a dozen wagons on his way to Charlottesville the previous week.[243] Here Lafayette recognized that he faced a potential threat from the British in that if he advanced directly southward with his troops, he would eventually approach Byrd's Tavern on the Three Chopt Road, which would be a poor defensive position from which to guard the Patriots' supply concentrations and to protect his army from nearby enemy forces. Instead, he elected to take up a location on the Three Chopt Road closer to Charlottesville and to move his soldiers in such a way as to avoid exposing his army at Byrd's Tavern, where part of Cornwallis's force was known to be posted.[244]

On the morning of June 12, Lafayette's troops left Boswell's Tavern and marched through thick piney woods "on nothing but a footpath, through which we got through with great difficulty," wrote a Pennsylvania officer. The army halted at a position astride the Three Chopt Road on the west side of Mechunk Creek, a small tributary of the Rivanna. In describing Lafayette's route to this advantageous position, most histories of the campaign give some variant of that provided by historian Henry P. Johnston in his 1881 study of the Yorktown Campaign: "Fortunately an old road, little known and long unused ran through the woods in the same direction [i.e., toward Mechunk Creek], and of this Lafayette promptly availed himself." The American troops improved the overgrown road in the darkness on the night of the eleventh and then, along with their artillery, made their way southeast early the next morning, reaching their defensive objective undetected by the enemy. "It appears Lord Cornwallis expected us where we did not intend

Lafayette's troops took up defensive positions on this high ground above Mechunk Creek in Fluvanna County to block British raids on American supply caches. *Author photgraph.*

to go," Lafayette wrote with some wry humor on June 12, adding with relief that "our stores are now behind us."[245] Later that month, he wrote to General Greene that it was both a "lucky march through a road little used" and "a stolen march thro' a difficult road."[246]

Located near the small wooden bridge over Mechunk Creek was a tavern previously operated by physician James Giles Allegre, who died in 1776. Lafayette's troops took up positions along the creek and around the tavern on the high ground on the west side of the bridge. Moreover, this location put Lafayette close to the main road leading south to Elk-hill and Point of Fork, which he could defend from his camp near the bridge if necessary.[247]

In this well-chosen spot, the Continentals and militiamen—along with some riflemen who had recently arrived in camp—dissuaded the British from pursuing further operations against Patriot military stores so that Cornwallis elected to march back to the Tidewater.[248] Cornwallis had "in vain endeavored to bring the Marquis to action," he informed General Leslie and, "having destroyed all stores within my reach," initiated his army's return to Richmond. Although a number of later histories state that the British remained at Elk-hill until June 15 or 16, contemporaries in the campaign—including Simcoe and Lafayette—indicate that the

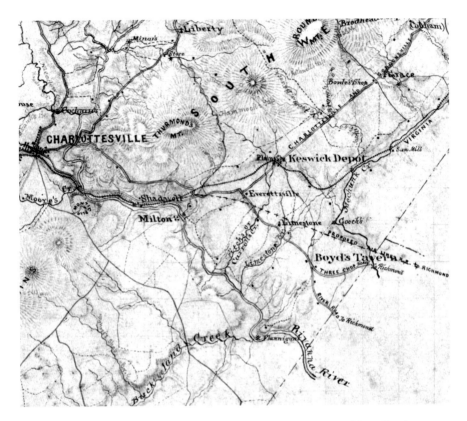

Detail of 1867 map showing Monticello, Milton, Shadwell and Three Chopt Road east of Charlottesville. Lafayette's defensive position at Mechunk Creek was where the word "Tavern" appears on the map's right edge. *Library of Congress.*

British troops began to leave Elk-hill late on the night of June 12–13.[249] The redcoats traveled along the River Road with Simcoe's cavalry as a rear guard and made camp around Goochland Court House on the evening of the thirteenth. The following day, they marched a dozen miles farther east and halted around a church and watermill on Dover Creek in eastern Goochland County. During the day's progress, the footsore redcoats and perhaps some of the runaway slaves in the rear sacked John Tayloe Griffin's home and seven-hundred-acre farm called Lightfoot's Beaverdam Plantation (later Mount Bernard) along the James River. According to Griffin, due to "the ravages of the British Army," he lost twelve slaves, several horses, tobacco, crops, 150 gallons of rum, molasses, salt, copper kettles and "a good wagon."[250]

Sending his wagons and unfit soldiers ahead under guard at midnight, Cornwallis had his troops moving early on June 15. The army passed

The modern bridge over Mechunk Creek. Lafayette's soldiers were posted on the far side of the shallow creek. *Author photograph.*

Tuckahoe but did not pillage it, and then it camped at Westham, near the ruins of the Virginia arms manufactory destroyed in January. The next day, the army arrived at Richmond, where it was soon joined by Tarleton's Legion, which had been strengthened by part of the Seventy-sixth Regiment on horseback and had moved east along the Three Chopt Road to "cover" Cornwallis's left flank as he advanced. These mounted troops had passed Napier's Mill and Peers Tavern in Goochland as they guarded the main column. While Cornwallis's troops remained at Richmond for several days, Simcoe's Rangers were posted at Westham, and Tarleton's command took up a position at Meadow Bridge on the Chickahominy River about seven miles north of Richmond.[251]

From Mechunk Creek, Lafayette had difficulty ascertaining Cornwallis's movements, due primarily to Tarleton's cavalry screen along Three Chopt Road. Some of the enemy's horse was still at Byrd's Ordinary on the thirteenth, when most of Cornwallis's men were on the march to Goochland Court House.[252]

Perhaps relived at having prevented further devastation by British troops, and being able to rest his men for a few days, Lafayette began to take stock of the campaign to date. "Virginia is not conquered and the American army…is not annihilated," he wrote.[253] He called the loss of supplies "very trifling" and "inconsiderable" and blamed the state assembly and Virginia's board of war for moving valuable arms to Charlottesville, "which upon the enemy's approach were left in their way." His army was still "much inferior to his Lordship," so he hesitated to risk much but noted that "what regular troops I have are very good but few in number."[254] He had placed his

The American Soldier, 1781. U.S. Army Center of Military History.

Continentals under Wayne in his "first line" and the state militia under the new governor, Thomas Nelson Jr., "the best that the state of Virginia could choose." His riflemen and light troops were under Muhlenberg, and with this small command, he had to face Cornwallis, who "has all the fine airs of an army."[255]

Lafayette expected additional reinforcements as well. In mid-June, militiamen—most armed with long rifles—began to arrive in the American camp from the Shenandoah Valley.[256] Lafayette scrambled to get more Virginia cavalrymen in his army as soon as they were equipped and sought to speed up the arrival of Colonel Steven Moylan's Continental dragoons, whom he hoped were on the way to join him by way of Fredericksburg.[257] General Weeden also wrote to Moylan in early June, imploring him to rush to Lafayette's camp. "Superiority of horse," Weeden noted, "gives the enemy a decided advantage and subjects his [Lafayette's] parties to every evil. In short, if he is not speedily reinforced they must overrun our country."[258]

In the days following the British cavalry raids against Continental and Virginia supply caches, Lafayette was particularly disappointed in the conduct of Baron von Steuben. He wrote to von Steuben from Allegre's Tavern, having heard that the baron was moving to the Staunton River, far to the south. He told von Steuben that Greene authorized him to stay in Virginia, not to proceed to the Carolinas as originally planned. Von Steuben had, in fact, been ordered by Greene to remain in Virginia, but as the orders were intercepted by an enemy patrol, he was unaware of the new directive. Lafayette informed the baron that Wayne's Continentals had joined him and that the combined forces were now in "a better situation" to defend the military supplies, which he ordered to "be removed higher up" toward the Blue Ridge Mountains. He asked von Steuben to return immediately to the James River and, with the Continentals and militia under his command, "hasten to form a junction with us."[259]

Although in his official correspondence, the marquis' descriptions of the baron's conduct at Point of Fork and afterward was restrained, privately he was exasperated. In a pique, Lafayette wrote to the Chevalier de la Luzerne, the French minister to the United States, that von Steuben had retreated eighty miles south from Point of Fork. The baron had taken up a position on the far side of the Staunton River at Cole's Ferry, far from the enemy, and seemed reluctant to return to the scene of action. Only the "remonstrances" of one of Lafayette's staff officers "and the militia's announcement that they would abandon him there" led von Steuben back to the James. "In every respect I have been, as we say, *disappointed*."[260]

Major General Baron von Steuben in 1783.
Library of Congress.

In a private letter to Washington in mid-June, Lafayette called the baron's conduct "unintelligible." Much of the criticism leveled against the Prussian drillmaster concerned his retreat from the banks of the James in the face of Simcoe's ruse and leaving supplies there to be destroyed. "Every man woman and child in Virginia is roused against him," Lafayette complained to his commander. "They dispute even of his courage, but I cannot believe their assertions." The Frenchman was upset that von Steuben

had 500 and odds new levies and some militia, that he was on the other side of a river which the freshet rendered very difficult to be crossed particularly by people that had no boats, that the greatest part of the accounts make Simcoe 400 strong half of them dragoons, that our stores on the south side were destroyed by about 30 or 40 men, that the baron went to Staunton River about 70 miles from the Point of Fork, that the militia abandoned him and I am informed the new levies deserted from him, because they did not like his maneuver. General Lawson and every officer and soldier both in the regulars and militia are so much exasperated against the Baron and cover him with so many ridicules that after I have obtained a junction with him I do not know where to employ him without giving offense. [261]

Von Steuben had abandoned an "unattackable position before so inferior a force, the reason of which no man of sense will be able to understand." [262] Several days later, he wrote to the French representative in Philadelphia that "the baron is so unpopular that I do not know where to put him," and to

Alexander Hamilton, he reported that "the hatred of the Virginians to him was truly hurtfull to the service."[263]

The French general was not the only one unhappy with von Steuben's conduct. Benjamin Harrison wrote just after Tarleton left Charlottesville that "his conduct gives universal disgust and injures the service much," adding that "I believe him a good officer on the parade but the worst in every other respect in the American Army."[264] Archibald Cary thought that "Baron Stuben deserves to be hanged for his Conduct." The state's House of Delegates called for an inquiry by Lafayette into the baron's conduct at the Point of Fork, but the Frenchman deflected the resolution. In late October, he wrote a letter to von Steuben complimenting his "great exertions and precision when present with me."[265]

Lafayette criticized von Steuben's march to Cole's Ferry, but the baron thought he was expected to join Greene's army. Moreover, von Steuben may also have feared that Tarleton's cavalry coming south from Charlottesville to Point of Fork would cross the James upriver and turn his left flank. After retreating in the night from Point of Fork, von Steuben moved on the Ampthill Road down the James to the mouth of the Willis River, near Carter's Ferry. From here, he brought his regulars and militia south to Cumberland Court House, and on the thirteenth, he arrived at Prince Edward Court House, fifty miles south of the James. By this time, von Steuben must have received word that he was expected to join Lafayette and not continue to the Carolinas. On the thirteenth, he advised Lafayette that he was collecting militia to augment the new Continental levies and planned to march them north to cross the James. The militia were "so slow turning out" that he asked North Carolina authorities for all armed militia they could send from the border of the two states to follow him into Virginia. He also wrote to the marquis that he had not received a letter from him since June 4 and from General Greene not since May 1.[266]

Lafayette not only looked to be reinforced by von Steuben but also expected troops raised and led by General Morgan to join him from the lower Shenandoah counties. On June 12, he wrote to Morgan appreciative of the "exertions you have made for our support. Your assistance is very necessary to us, and your success in collecting troops is even above my expectations." Indicative of how important it was to gather well-equipped troops, Lafayette gave Morgan authority to do what he thought best "for the good of the service" and have it "executed in my name."[267]

Either on the afternoon of June 13 or the following day, Lafayette must have received word of Cornwallis's march to Richmond, as he decided to move his own troops east to Byrd's Ordinary early on the fourteenth. The men marched through a "d[amne]d poor country, the water being very scarce," a Continental officer complained, and another soldier wrote that the troops walked "ten miles through so poor a country it did not produce one drop of water." Following the redcoats at a safe distance, "we make it seem we are pursuing him," the marquis quipped to the Chevalier de la Luzerne. "When he [Cornwallis] moves from one place to another," he continued, "I try to let my movements give his the appearance of a retreat. Would to God there were a way to give him the appearance of a defeat." He added that "Lord Cornwallis seemed not to like these hilly terrains" of the Piedmont.[268]

On the fifteenth, the American troops crossed Roundabout Creek east of Byrd's Ordinary and then stopped several miles farther on to camp at Fork Creek (in Louisa County) after "a very fatiguing march." This encampment was probably north of Three Chopt Road since the marquis was wary of getting too close to Cornwallis's rear guard under Tarleton on that road and the American army was headed toward Dandridge's Plantation on the South Anna River.[269] He reported his pleasure of having western Virginia riflemen, "their faces smeared with charcoal," with him, making "the woods resound with their yells; I have made them an army of devils and have given them plenary absolution," the marquis noted.[270]

Lafayette's route to Dandridge's is not known, but letters and maps show that his army arrived at Deep Creek by June 16 as it marched east. As this was a stream not crossed by Three Chopt Road, it appears that the marquis' troops were marching in Louisa County close to the South Anna River, perhaps along the Old Mountain Road, which Jack Jouett might have followed on his overnight ride to Charlottesville.[271]

Halting temporarily at Deep Creek, Lafayette reported to General Weedon on the sixteenth that his troops were following Cornwallis's army toward Richmond and that he intended to proceed to Dandridge's Plantation. He told Weedon to "hurry" all militia companies in the field south of the Rappahannock to his army since many of his militia soldiers "are going home, and no relief [was] coming." He requested lead, cartridges, shoes and rum. "The water of this country is very unhealthy to the northern soldiers," so "a large supply of vinegar and rum would be very welcome." Lafayette told Weeden to transport these items using "military impress" if need be: "Upon your execution my dear sir and upon decided measures is all my dependence."[272]

Weedeon replied to Lafayette on the seventeenth from Fredericksburg to advise him that shoes were hard to come by as "all the stores and factories

Oldfield, Colonel Nathaniel Dandridge's home on Turkey Creek, is where Lafayette's troops camped twice during the 1781 campaign, near modern Vontay. *Author photograph.*

in and near this place were sent away on the first [reports] of the enemies advance." He had written to both General Morgan and Colonel Moyland of the Fourth Continental Dragoons urging them to come forward from Pennsylvania soon to join the army and to collect shoes as they marched through the countryside. He was also taking steps to procure more arms for Lafayette's soldiers, but a "lack of lead has prevented my having a supply of cartridges at this place."[273]

On June 17, Lafayette's troops reached Dandridge's Plantation and encamped along Allen's and Turkey Creeks, and the marquis likely made his headquarters in the colonel's still extant brick home called Oldfield along Turkey Creek. The day's march had been "through the best country we have ever seen in this state," wrote an impressed Pennsylvania officer.[274] Here, Lafayette was gathering a significant force, centered on his own 800 light infantry, Wayne's troops, now reduced to 700 men, 50 tolerably appointed dragoons and his artillery. Von Steuben arrived at Dandridge's on June 18 or 19 with about 450 new Continental recruits, although the baron himself soon left the army temporarily due to poor health. Joining the marquis as well were 800 to 900 riflemen under Virginia's newly appointed brigadier general William Campbell, whom Lafayette regarded as an officer "whose service must have endeared him to every citizen, and particularly to every American soldier." Additionally, 2,000 militiamen under the overall command of General Nelson were included in his total strength of about 5,000 men.[275]

On June 18, Lafayette attempted to strike Tarleton's outpost near Meadow Bridge, a dozen miles away at John Norrel's Ordinary. He sent forth General Muhlenberg's light troops, supported by part of his Continental troops under General Wayne, from Dandridge's Plantation "to cut them off and make sure work of it." Tarleton's troopers, however, were alerted to the Americans' advance "by some rascals having given them information of our movement," and the British "precipitately retreated to Richmond." The American troops retired four miles away, "where we lay destitute of any refreshment, bedding or covering."[276]

On June 20, the marquis posted his troops a few miles north, toward the South Anna River around Mount Brilliant. That day the British left Richmond and marched east to Bottoms Bridge, which they reached on the twenty-first. Having received intelligence about the enemy's evacuation of Virginia's capital, Lafayette advised Wayne that if the British were "near us this would be a good time for a night attack." Wayne was to follow the redcoats by "whatever road they took," and if "opportunity offers to attack them you will do for the best." General Muhlenberg's mounted light infantry operated in front of Wayne's pursuit of Cornwallis.[277]

Lafayette was still wary of the British host, even with his increased numbers, as "the fate of the southern states depends on the preservation of this army," and therefore a defeat had to be avoided.[278] Coincidently, Greene wrote Lafayette two days later from South Carolina along the same lines. "Avoid a general action if possible," he advised the young French nobleman, "a defeat to you in that situation may prove your ruin." Later that day, the army marched southeast to Sims Mill and then eight miles farther to halt at "Burrill's Ornery, destitute of every necessary of life," an exhausted officer recalled.[279]

On June 22, Lafayette moved his headquarters and some of his troops to a location he called Process, actually the plantation and water mill of Thomas Prosser in Henrico County on North Run, a short distance upstream from Brook's Bridge.[280] Late that afternoon, he ordered von Steuben, four miles to his rear, to march his troops six or seven miles that night and then proceed east the following morning by way of Savage's, north of Bottoms Bridge along the Williamsburg Road, where he was to join the rest of Lafayette's and Wayne's forces.[281]

At the same time, he sent a message to Wayne ordering him to close up on Muhlenberg's light troops, which were nearer to the enemy's rear. Lafayette wished for Wayne to reinforce Muhlenberg with two hundred mounted Continentals led by Colonel Richard Butler of the Fifth Pennsylvania, whom he held in high regard, in order to impede the British column prior

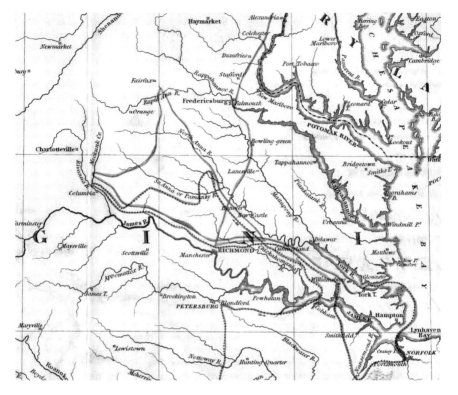

This early postwar map shows the movements of the British and American forces, including Cornwallis's route to Yorktown. *Library of Congress.*

to an attack.[282] Wayne received this message six hours later and quickly replied to his chief. His men had marched twenty-two miles that day and "nature therefore requires some respite as well as substance." Despite their exhaustion, Wayne promised to have his men on the road chasing after the British at two o'clock the next morning, June 23. He apologized that he had not made the night attack that Lafayette had suggested the day before, as he received the orders too late to do so. He suggested that he join Muhlenberg's force so "that we might act with some prospect of success," which he thought the army deserved. "You'll have the goodness to excuse [the] ardour of a soldier," he concluded his letter.[283]

Wayne's Continentals passed through Richmond on June 22. Many houses there had been ruined by the British, a Pennsylvania officer observed, and the invaders had "destroyed a great quantity of tobacco, which they threw into the streets and set fire to it."[284] It was "a scene of much distress," another of Wayne's soldiers observed. The American troops halted for the night on

Gilles Creek, east of the town below Church Hill on the Williamsburg Road. The following morning, the troops set off at 2:00 a.m., and when resting six hours later, "we had an alarm." Major Ebenezer Denny of the Pennsylvania Continentals wrote that "near Bacon's [Bottoms?] Bridge the British turned upon us; our advance pressed them too close." Lieutenant Feltman of the Pennsylvania line also recorded the events in his journal:

> *Our Light Horse brought us intelligence that the enemy was within one mile of us. The army immediately formed for action and an universal joy prevailed, that certain success was before us. We lay on our arms ten hours, hourly receiving accounts of their advance…but to our great mortification it turned out to be a false alarm.*

Major Denny wrote that the soldiers had been "formed for a fight" and that Wayne was "very anxious to do something," but the enemy "did not come on." That night at about midnight, "a very heavy rain came on," drenching the weary troops, who had no tents to shelter them.[285]

The next morning was a "fine" one, and the American troops with Wayne remained in camp "all day enjoying ourselves and cooking," as well as drying out their muskets and uniforms. On a more somber note, one of the Continentals from the Fourth Pennsylvania was apprehended after trying to desert to the enemy, tried by a brigade court-martial "and executed in the evening" by a firing squad. After dusk, the troops marched east twelve miles "in order to surprise Tarleton" in James City County, but "he got wind of our approach and retired."[286]

At some point on the twenty-third, von Steuben's troops caught up with Wayne's Continentals along the Williamsburg Road.[287] These Continental recruits were now led by Colonel Christian Febiger, a native of Denmark who had settled near Boston before the war, had been captured during the disastrous Quebec campaign of 1775 and had worked tirelessly in 1780 and 1781 to forward supplies to the Southern Department from Philadelphia. Also in late June, one hundred men in six troops of the Fourth Continental Light Dragoons under Colonel Moyland joined Wayne's command in Virginia.[288]

Lafayette correctly surmised that Cornwallis was heading for Williamsburg. After leaving Richmond and crossing Bottoms Bridge, the British reached New Kent Court House on June 22, several miles south of the winding Pamunkey River. The main body of Cornwallis's army reached Williamsburg on the twenty-fifth after the redcoats "destroyed some cannon and stores as they passed through the country." Tarleton acted as a rear

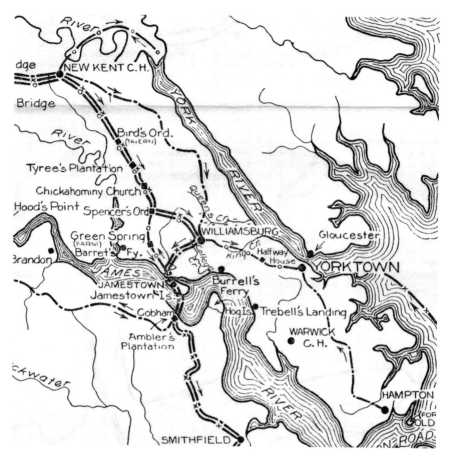

A 1930s map detail of the area between New Kent and Hampton. *From Landers, Yorktown 1781.*

guard "inclining toward the Pamunkey" while Simcoe operated to the south of Cornwallis's long column of troops, wagons, artillery and runaway slaves. All the while, Tarleton wrote, Lafayette used his light troops and regulars "to hang upon the rear."[289]

"WE WAGE WAR LIKE GENTLEMEN"

Two Battles and the Path to Yorktown

Of dry top'd oaks they seem'd two forests thick,
So did each host with spears and pikes abound:
Bent were their bows, in rest their lances stick,
Their hands shook swords, their slings held cobles round.
—"A Face-off in the Crusades," Torquato Tasso, sixteenth century

Having followed the British closely since the middle of June, part of Lafayette's army finally caught up with an enemy detachment six miles west of Williamsburg. Cornwallis had sent Simcoe with the Queen's Rangers and some Hessian jaegers to forage and destroy additional supplies and vessels along the Chickahominy River. The marquis learned of Simcoe's expedition and planned to cut off the young dragoon colonel as his small force retired to Williamsburg. For this operation, he employed Colonel Butler's Pennsylvania Regiment, two companies of riflemen, and over fifty cavalrymen under Major William McPherson, all commanded by Butler. These troops moved quickly through the night of June 25 "in full speed" and, on the way, encountered a "negro man with the small pox lying on the road side," left there by Simcoe "to prevent the Virginia militia from pursuing them, which the enemy frequently did." On the next morning, these American troops encountered Simcoe's force halted at Spencer's Ordinary, along the Williamsburg Road near its intersection with the Jamestown Road, near what was called Hot Water Plantation by many Virginia militiamen.[290]

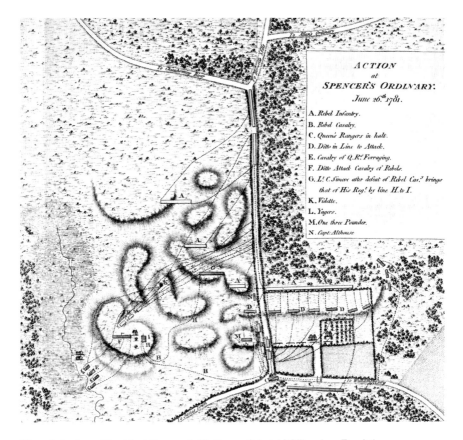

Plan of the June skirmish at Spencer's Ordinary. *Colonial Williamsburg Foundation.*

McPherson attacked with about fifty of his dragoons and fifty mounted New Jersey light infantrymen and quickly drove in Simcoe's pickets. Simcoe counterattacked on the American right flank, and in the "severe skirmish," McPherson was thrown from his mount, although he managed to escape while the rest of his horsemen were scattered. Simcoe claimed that McPherson "crept into a swamp, lay there unperceived during the action, and when it was over got off." From captives taken on the field, Simcoe learned that more Patriot troops were nearby, so he called to Cornwallis for reinforcements.[291]

Soon the Virginia rifle companies arrived at the scene and engaged in a hot, confusing firefight with the Queen's Rangers, who gradually pushed them back to the lines of Butler's Pennsylvanians. Wayne, meanwhile, sent more of his Pennsylvania troops forward to support Butler's attack. Sensing his predicament, Simcoe deployed his force to make it appear larger and then withdrew, leaving his wounded on the field and by the tavern after two hours of fighting. Butler's men fell back on Wayne's Continentals around Byrd's Ordinary and then to Lafayette's camp at Tyree's Plantation, where the American forces stayed until July 5, on the west side of Diascund Creek. Some of the American wounded were brought to a military hospital at New Kent Court House.[292]

Lafayette reported on the action to Governor Nelson two days later:

> *Colonel Simcoe was so lucky as to avoid a part of the stroke; but altho' the whole of the* [American] *light corps could not arrive in time, some of them did. Majr. MacPherson having taken up fifty light infantry, behind fifty dragoons overtook Simcoe, and regardless,* [illegible] *of numbers made an immediate charge. He was supported by the rifle-men who behaved most gallantly and did great execution. The alarm guns were fired at Williamsburg (only six miles distant from the field). A detachment just then going to Gloucester was recalled, and the whole British army came out to save Simcoe. They retired next morning when our army got within striking distance.*[293]

Cornwallis brought his troops west and met Simcoe, with whom he returned to secure the wounded and claim possession of the field. The marquis, who regarded the affair as a victory, reported his losses as nine killed, fourteen wounded and "one Lieut. [and] 12 privates whose fate is not known." He claimed sixty British were killed, "which must be attributed to the great skill of our rifle-men," but Cornwallis reported far fewer losses. Nevertheless, Lafayette noted that "his little success has given great satisfaction to the troops, and increased their ardor."[294]

In late June, Lafayette's command included 850 of his light infantry detachment, 600 Pennsylvania Continentals under Wayne, 400 Virginia Continental recruits and 120 dragoons. Shoes, medicine, "hard money," arms and cavalry equipment were sorely lacking within his army, however, and he still needed more horsemen. Although he expected to have almost 3,000 militiamen with him soon, many of these Virginians began to leave the ranks as their terms expired and as harvest time began to draw near.[295] By early July, the marquis found that "the three [militia] brigades are so amazingly reduced that to have them of a tolerable strength I have been obliged to put them into two," under Generals Lawson and Edward Stevens. Desertions were increasing, with many men saying "they were only engaged for six weeks and the harvest time recalls them home," even the western

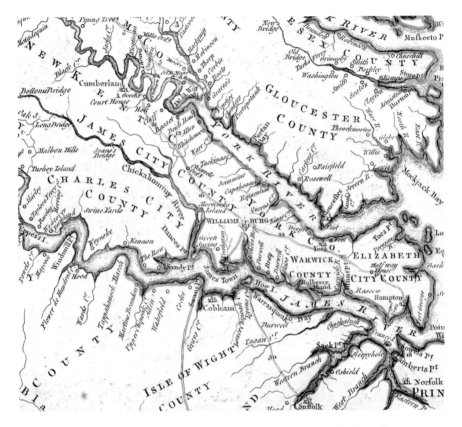

Map detail of the area between Bottom's Bridge and Norfolk, where both armies maneuvered in July and August 1781. *North Carolina Collection, University of North Carolina–Chapel Hill.*

riflemen. "You might as well stop the flood tide as stop militia whose times are out," Lafayette complained. The Frenchman called on the governor to immediately muster dragoons and thousands more soldiers from the militia as "an absolute necessity," as well as a unit of black pioneers and wagoneers, who would "afford great services" to the army.[296]

In the beginning of July, Lafayette's four thousand troops were in several dispersed camps northwest of Williamsburg, where Cornwallis's redcoats retired after the skirmish at Spencer's Ordinary. "We never encamp in a body," Lafayette wrote to General Greene, taking precaution not to present an inviting target for Cornwallis to attack. He expected Morgan's newly raised command to join him, though it was only four hundred men. "Our movements are offensive and we appear eager for action," he told Greene.[297]

By this time Cornwallis's operations had taken on a defensive quality compared to his destructive expedition in May and June. "The enemy are extremely cautious," Lafayette concluded on the fourth, suspecting that the British general would embark his troops and leave the state, except perhaps for a small garrison at Portsmouth. Lafayette intended to keep his distance from Williamsburg, watch his own flanks and prevent the enemy from making foraging detachments. Still, the young French general was frustrated. "I do what I can, but cannot do what I wish," he confided to Greene, concluding that "I manage matters for the best, try to correct abuses, get angry five or six times a day, and I hope you will be satisfied at least with my good intentions."[298]

Upon Cornwallis's arrival in Williamsburg on June 25, he received two June letters from Sir Henry Clinton in New York. Clinton was concerned that Washington and his French allies were preparing an assault on New York by land and sea, which could overwhelm its garrison of eleven thousand men. Clinton directed Cornwallis to secure a favorable port in the Chesapeake region to establish a defensive post and ordered him to send three thousand of his troops to New York, once active operations had concluded. Cornwallis quickly readied his troops to move eastward to Portsmouth, wary of Lafayette's army, which he suspected had "an intention of insulting our rearguard when we pass James River." His lordship planned to cross the river around James Town, first striking at the Americans if he saw "a favorable opportunity," but he also warned Clinton that he saw "little chance of being able to establish a post capable of giving effectual protection to ships of war" in Virginia's coastal area.[299]

On July 4, the British left Williamsburg and marched south to a camp at Humbler's (or Ambler's) Plantation near James Town Island in order to cross to the south side of the river. The Queen's Rangers crossed the James that night and moved to Cobham, a small town in Surry County at the mouth of Grays Creek that no longer exists. Cornwallis moved his baggage and stores across on the fifth and intended to move all his troops across the river on July 7.[300]

Lafayette learned that Cornwallis left Virginia's old capital on the fifth. The marquis moved his own troops to Byrd's Tavern and Norrell's Mill on Yarmouth Creek, just east of the Chickahominy River, and then occupied a position for a few days beginning July 6 at Chickahominy Church, about ten miles west of Williamsburg. In an attempt to reconnoiter the location of Cornwallis's troops at the vulnerable position crossing the James, Lafayette ordered on the sixth an advance detachment numbering eight hundred men under General Wayne to scout the enemy near James Town. These troops

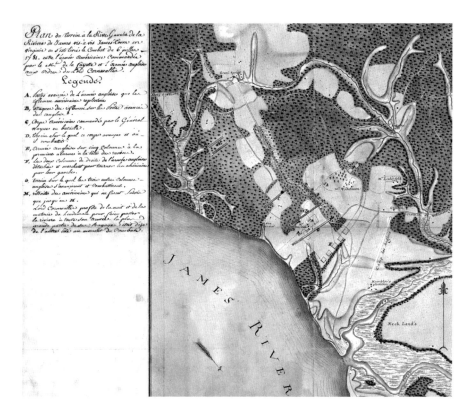

French map of the battle at Green Spring, fought near Jamestown on July 6, 1781. *Library of Congress.*

included the Pennsylvania Continentals, militia riflemen and three guns. "Nothing but a forced march with the lightest & most advanced part of the troops could arrive in time to effect their rear," Wayne wrote. He found the enemy's camp pickets near Green Spring, a large plantation dating from the mid-seventeenth century, a few miles northwest of James Town. The old plantation still included the large brick house that had been the residence of Virginia governor William Berkeley in the 1670s and was described just after the Revolution as "a brick building of great solidity, but no attempt at grandeur."[301]

Cornwallis learned of Wayne's approach to the river and planned to surprise the rebels by concealing most of his army from the American general's view, thereby leading Wayne to believe that most of the British force had already crossed the James and only a token force remained near James Town Island. The three Pennsylvania battalions advanced in line to within eighty yards on the redcoats' position "under a very heavy fire of grape shot." As the sun began to set, Wayne attacked the British cavalry outposts south of Green Spring with his riflemen. Cornwallis allowed Wayne's troops to move near his lines, "concluding that [Wayne] would not bring a considerable force within our reach, unless they supposed that nothing was left but a rear guard."[302]

While Wayne's soldiers exchanged "a smart firing" with the enemy, Lafayette came on the field with additional Continentals and seems to have suspected that the British had more than a rear guard fighting Wayne's men.[303] "It was soon discovered," Wayne wrote, "that a very considerable part of their army yet remained on this side [of] the river [at Ambler's] which induced the General [Lafayette] to send for the remainder of the Continentals distant about Six miles." Wayne described the most significant engagement of the campaign in detail to General Washington two days later.

At 2 OClock P.M. a large smoke was raised by the Enemy, probably as a signal to their parties to return to camp, & for all such as had crossed the river to repass it, at 3 OClock the rifle men supported by a few regulars began & kept up a galling fire upon the Enemy which continued until five in the Evening when the British began to move forward in five Columns[.] The Marquis anxious to view them near had proceeded rather far upon their left, it was then thought proper to Order Major [William] Galvan of the head of the advance guard to meet & attack their front who after a spirited tho' unequal contest retired upon our left[.] A Detachment of the Light Infantry under Major [John] Willis [Wyllys], having that moment arrived also commenced a severe fire upon the Enemies left but were obliged to fall back, which the enemy taking advantage of & beginning to turn our flanks, a <u>Manoeuvre</u> in which had they persevered, they must inevitably penetrated between this Corps & the Other part of the army; but being joined at this Crisis by Lieut Colo. [Josiah] Harmer & Major Edwards with two Detachments from the 2nd & 3rd Battalions of Penns[ylvani]ans under Colo. [Richard] Hampton, it was determined among <u>a Choice of Difficulties</u> to advance & Charge them[.] This was done with such vivacity as to produce the desired effect i.e. checking them in their advance & diverting them from their first maneuver.[304]

Wayne reported that "being enveloped by [superior] numbers [and] many brave & worthy Officers & soldiers killed or wounded, we found it expedient to fall back half a mile" to Green Spring plantation. Two of the Continental six-pounder field pieces that "were served with equal spirit & effect, until disabled by having Captain [Jesse] Crosby with many matrosses dangerously wounded & all the horses killed, at last fell into their hands." One of Wayne's officers wrote that "our artillery horses being nearly all killed or wounded, we were obliged to abandon our two pieces of artillery which fell into the enemies hands." Wayne managed to retire safely with his wagons and ammunition, and after falling back one mile, his infantrymen managed to reform "and retired in good order."[305]

British officers, unsurprisingly, reported the affair somewhat differently. Tarleton recalled that the first cannon shot of the Americans was the forward dragoons' signal to withdraw and for the infantry to form and advance. Cornwallis reported that Lafayette "intended to attack our rear-guard, and luckily stumbled on our army." The British commander "put the troops under arms and ordered the army to advance in two lines. The attack was begun by the first line with great spirit." In his front line, the light infantry advanced on the right, and on his left, he sent forward Lieutenant Colonel Dundas's brigade, consisting of the Forty-third, Seventy-sixth and Eightieth Regiments, against Wayne's Continentals and two field guns. Soon, "a smart action ensued for some minutes," and Wayne's hard-pressed battalions began to get enveloped by the longer lines of redcoats coming against him. Upon perceiving that he was almost surrounded, Wayne ordered a bayonet charge against the enemy line in his front, which temporarily checked the British advance and gave time for Wayne's force to retreat to the lines of the American light troops, one half mile to the rear. Although Cornwallis's troops had forced the Americans back, they failed to deliver the telling blow his Lordship anticipated would destroy most of Lafayette's command. "The darkness of the evening prevented me from making use of the cavalry, or it is probable the Pennsylvania line would have been demolished," his lordship reported. British losses were eleven killed, sixty-six wounded and one missing.[306]

Most of Lafayette's troops returned to Chickahominy Church, while the militia at Byrd's Ordinary moved forward to support the regulars. The marquis reported losses of twenty-eight killed, ninety-nine wounded and twelve missing, including Colonel John Bowyer of the rifle battalion from Rockbridge County, taken prisoner during the action.[307] "The services rendered by the officers make me happy to think that although many were wounded, we lost none," wrote the marquis. He was proud that Wayne's command "attacked the whole British Army, close to their encampment, and by this severe skirmish hastened their retreat." To Washington, he wrote that Cornwallis "seems to have given up the conquest of Virginia."[308]

Wayne's report to Washington was boastful and sought to put a positive face on events at Green Spring. He noted that

> *our small reconnoitering party of Horse & foot who had the hardiness to engage Lord Cornwallis at the head of His Whole army with the Advantage of so Numerous a Cavalry on their own ground & in their own Camp, is more to be envied than pitied—as it not only disconcerted the British General & effectually aroused him from his premeditated maneuver, but precipitated his retreat to James Island the same night to avoid a Genl action in the morning, which the pointed attack he experienced in the Evening might be the sanguinary prelude to.*

The Pennsylvania general also noted that Lafayette lost two horses during the battle, in which the marquis was exposed to enemy musketry at the front of his men. "He was frequently requested to keep at a greater Distance," Wayne reported, but "his Native bravery rendered him deaf to the Admonition."[309]

From the battlefield, where Lafayette moved the majority of his command by July 8, he congratulated Wayne's command for their bravery against the "total of the British Army" in "a warm and close action."[310] Although Cornwallis moved all of his troops across the James on July 7, Lafayette knew better than to think the British commander was retreating. In a letter to the Vicomte de Noailles, another French officer serving in America, he wrote candidly about his wily opponent. "This devil Cornwallis is much wiser than the other generals with whom I have dealt," wrote the marquis, "he inspires me with a sincere fear, and his name has greatly troubled my sleep. This campaign is a good school for me. God grant that the public does not pay for my lessons."[311]

In fact, the American public did *not* pay for Lafayette's military education. When the British moved to the south bank of the James, the marquis withdrew his forces west from Green Spring back toward Bottoms Bridge and Richmond and did not pursue the redcoats on their march to Suffolk. The sharp contest at Green Spring, the only significant engagement between the forces of Cornwallis and Lafayette during their 1781 maneuvers in the Tidewater and Piedmont of Virginia, marked the end of the two generals' cat-and-mouse game. To be sure, the campaign was not over—Cornwallis and his powerful host still threatened the state from Portsmouth. Lafayette too remained in Virginia, close enough to the enemy to keep a watchful eye on British operations while securing as much of the Old Dominion as possible with his smaller forces. Meanwhile, far to the north at Washington's headquarters at Newburgh, New York, and

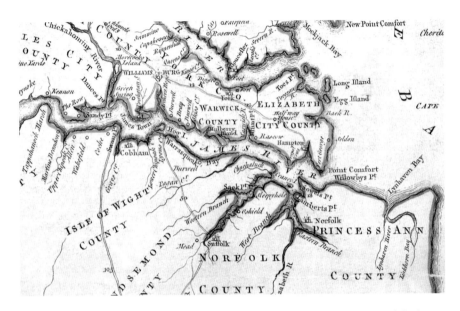

Lower James River region around Norfolk, Suffolk and Yorktown. *North Carolina Collection, University of North Carolina–Chapel Hill.*

in French camps in Rhode Island and Connecticut, plans were being made to bring thousands of troops and ships to Virginia to capture the king's forces along the wide rivers of coastal Virginia.

After the battle at Green Spring, the British troops crossed James River on July 7 with "great labor and difficulty," and Cornwallis moved southeast to Suffolk by July 12. With General Leslie's assistance, he began preparing to send back part of his command from Portsmouth to New York, per Clinton's repeated orders, which Cornwallis finally received upon his arrival at Suffolk.[312]

Soon, however, the British commander in New York changed his mind. Clinton sought to establish a station in the Chesapeake region for ships of the line, which the current British post at Portsmouth could not accommodate, and he favored Hampton Roads. After consulting with Rear Admiral Thomas Graves, who replaced Arbuthnot as commander of the North American Squadron in May, Clinton told Cornwallis in July not to abandon Virginia, but to remain on the defensive, and to consider Yorktown or Old Point Comfort (Hampton) as a possible deep-water port for British warships. Specifically, in a July 11 letter, he ordered Cornwallis not to send the troops he previously requested to New York.[313]

If Virginians thought they no longer had to fear the destructiveness of British arms as Cornwallis moved to the coast, they were mistaken. On

July 8, Cornwallis ordered Tarleton to strike out from Cobham for "an excursion" along the south side of the James River, with his dragoons and the light company of the Royal Welch Fusiliers.[314] Cornwallis concluded that since most of the Continental and Virginia forces were on the lower James with little opportunity to cross the river due to their lack of boats, "I thought it a good opportunity to endeavor to destroy the magazines between James River and the Dan," which were being gathered for the use of Greene's army in South Carolina. Tarleton was to aim for the depots at Prince Edward Court House and New London, the latter in far-off Bedford County. "All persons of consequence, civil or military," were to be brought to Cornwallis's headquarters "before they are paroled." To Tarleton, he wrote that while on this raid "you will be in no haste to return but do everything in your power to destroy the supplies destined for the rebel army." At the same time, Cornwallis sent part of the Eightieth Regiment under Colonel Dundas south to destroy rebel supplies at South Quay, in Southampton County on the Blackwater River, and "if possible I shall send a detachment to Edenton [North Carolina] for the same purpose before I fall back to Portsmouth."[315]

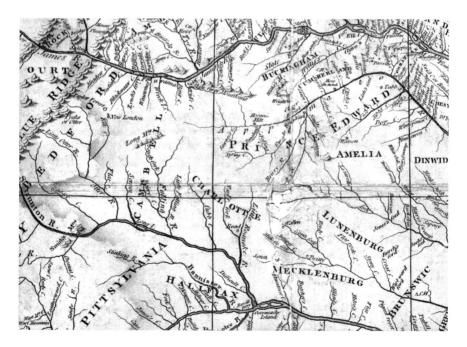

Key sites of Tarleton's Southside raid are depicted in this colonial period map, including New London, Amelia and Jefferson's Poplar Forest. *Library of Congress.*

Tarleton and his expeditionary force passed through Petersburg on their way west to Amelia. He "proceeded by long movements in the morning and evening," in order to avoid the heat of the summer and give his troops "refreshment and repose." At Benjamin Ward's Tavern along West Creek in southern Amelia County, several of his troopers skirmished with Peter Francisco, a rebel veteran of several previous battles during the war and known for his great size and courage. Francisco wrote a dramatic account of the affair in the third person decades after the war:

> *He fell in accidently, at the house of Benjamin Ward, in Amelia county, Va., with a plundering party of British detached from the main body of Tarleton's command, who came to Ward's for plunder, he* [Francisco] *being at Ward's when they came, and not having time to escape. One of the British demanded his watch and some other jewelry that he owned, and also at the same time placed his sword under his right arm, whilst disposing of the other property. He stepped back one pace in the rear, seized his sword by the hilt, cut off a large portion of his skull and killed him. He had then neither sword nor pistol of his own, but fought with his adversary's own weapons, which he took from him. He wounded and drove off the others, and took eight horses, with their trappings, out of nine; the ninth man escape*[d] *with a large cut on his back. They all joined Tarleton, who was about a mile off, except the slain man. This was the last favor I ever did the British.*

Francisco made his escape from the tavern on one of the enemy's mounts, driving the others before him.[316]

After riding through Amelia County, the dragoons traveled south by way of Jenning's Ordinary and Burke's Tavern (Burkeville). They next went to Prince Edward Court House, site of a gunpowder manufactory, and Charlotte Court House and then to the supply depot at New London. With an arsenal, a prison and three hundred inhabitants, the town was also the site of the first courthouse of Bedford County, beginning in 1761. Coincidently, Thomas Jefferson was then residing at his Poplar Forest estate only seven miles to the north of New London, but Tarleton did not capture him.[317]

At Prince Edward Court House and New London the British were disappointed to find that most of the military stores thought to be located at these depots had been previously sent to Greene's army. Throughout the raid, Tarleton discovered that "the stores destroyed, either of a public or private nature, were not in quantity or value equivalent to the damage sustained in

Peter Francisco fought off a detachment of Tarleton's dragoons in Amelia County in July 1781. *Library of Congress.*

the skirmishes en route, and the loss of men and horses by the excessive heat of the climate."[318] The dragoons returned east toward Cornwallis's position by a different route and, along the way, burned Reverend James Craig's mill, a supply depot and a "public magazine" on Flat Rock Creek in Lunenburg County. Tradition holds that Tarleton forced Reverend Craig, "though in poor health," to help slaughter pigs for the British soldiers' provisions and took off most of his slaves. Craig and many of his neighbors "were greatly injured in their property," according to a petition they sent to Governor Nelson soon after the enemy had departed, "and compelled" to sign paroles "when taken from their own homes."[319]

Tarleton's column, "almost destitute of necessities and accoutrements," rode east across Virginia's Southside to the Nottaway River at Walker's Mill in Brunswick County and then trotted along on the Boydton Road through Dinwiddie Court House, "with many unfavorable circumstances to the corps." The British dragoon colonel must have been aware that some of Lafayette's troops under Wayne had moved to western Chesterfield County and tried to avoid them. Even so, the British sustained casualties in several skirmishes with militia forces on their return route. After halting at Prince George Court House, Tarleton brought his troops along the James River to meet Cornwallis's main body at Suffolk, about seventy miles southeast, probably by way of Surrey Court House and Smithfield. Tarleton's command had been gone fifteen days and ridden over four hundred miles. Once Tarleton united with Cornwallis on July 24, his lordship marched his men to Portsmouth.[320]

North of the James, Lafayette repositioned his troops. After the contest at Green Spring, Lafayette moved his wounded to New Kent and marched west from Williamsburg to Holt's Forge and Long Bridge along the Chickahominy River, reaching Richmond by July 15. A few days before this, he ordered General Wayne to reinforce General Greene in the Carolinas with his five hundred Pennsylvania Continentals and the three hundred recruits von Steuben had raised in June. The marquis decided to detach this "much reduced" force because of his belief that Cornwallis would soon send most or all of his forces to New York or South Carolina.[321]

Lafayette also learned of Tarleton's mounted expedition south of the James and worried about supply caches all over the southern Piedmont. "From the best intelligence I can get the enemy's cavalry are gone very high up the country," he informed Wayne. Lafayette authorized "a stroke at Colonel Tarleton" if "found practicable" by Wayne, whom he expected to join General Morgan's troops at Goode's Bridge, a crossing of the Appomattox River between Chesterfield and Amelia Counties. He suggested that Governor Nelson call out enough militia to "render their return a very hazardous maneuver" south of City Point, but this was not realized.[322] Wayne's command crossed the James River at Woodson's Ferry on July 16 and then marched to Ware Bottom Church at Bermuda Hundred in Chesterfield County. Three days later, the troops arrived at Goode's Bridge, where they joined Morgan's riflemen and some Maryland cavalry troopers. Because the British had not embarked their forces at Portsmouth as Lafayette expected, Wayne's troops remained here until July 30, when they, fatigued by very hot weather, crossed the Appomattox into Amelia County.[323]

At Malvern Hill east of Richmond, Lafayette's remaining militia troops were encamped and resting in a healthy position. His most reliable troops were still the light infantry, "the best troops that ever took the field…far superior to any British troops." Lafayette boasted that these Continentals "saved this state, and indeed the southern part of the Continent." Additionally, some militia companies were at Williamsburg, and the Gloucester County militiamen were "in their own County." Some three hundred militia units remained on the south of the James River as well, ordered by the marquis "to keep clear of danger from an attack."[324] Despite being in no imminent danger from Cornwallis, still at Portsmouth, Lafayette continued to trouble state and Continental authorities to collect well-equipped cavalry for his host. "Upon my word," he wrote in late July, "unless we have a cavalry the defense of this state wholly depends upon the mistakes of our enemy."[325]

Lafayette was still trying to discern what the enemy's intentions were. Some of the redcoats had boarded transport ships and were off Hampton Roads but had yet to sail. The marquis considered that their intended destination was New York or Charles Town but could not rule out an expedition up the Potomac or to Baltimore. Cornwallis was observed inspecting Old Point Comfort by local spies, surely an indication he was considering fortifying that point. Baffled, the marquis ordered Wayne to move his troops back toward the James River opposite Manakin (in eastern Goochland County) in early August.[326]

In the lower Chesapeake, meanwhile, the British were active in late July. Cornwallis found Old Point Comfort unacceptable as a port for large ships. Accordingly, he decided to abandon Portsmouth and, instead, fortify Yorktown and the small peninsula opposite the town, Gloucester Point, obeying what he considered to be Clinton's orders. British forces arrived on the York River and occupied both Yorktown and Gloucester Point during

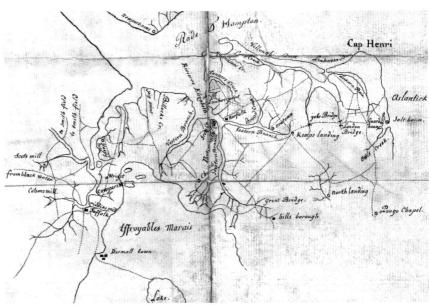

Hampton Roads and Norfolk map detail. *Library of Congress.*

the first two days of August and completed the evacuation of their defenses at Portsmouth on August 18. The British took a large number of runaway slaves with them, but "a number of Negroes" were "left dead and dying with the small pox." Redcoats, Hessians and former slaves began the laborious construction of defenses at both Yorktown and Gloucester Point, where they would remain until disaster struck in mid-October at the hands of a combined American and French army.[327]

Lafayette received prompt reports of the British movement and began to shift his own forces accordingly. He moved his command from Malvern Hill to Brook's Bridge, north of the capital, and then to Newcastle on the Pamunkey River by August 4, which allowed him to guard against a possible enemy thrust against Fredericksburg. General Wayne marched north, crossed the James River with his troops on August 5 at Westham and marched through Richmond to a position near Bottoms Bridge on the ninth. By August 11, Lafayette had moved his force over the Pamunkey at Ruffin's Ferry and then went on to Colonel Bernard Moore's Romancoke Plantation between the Pamunkey and Mattaponi Rivers in eastern King William County near West Point, where fodder and provisions were more plentiful. Lafayette also collected there numerous boats for transporting supplies to his camp and for anticipated troop movements. He remained until August 30,

Nineteenth-century view of the Pamunkey River, along which Lafayette's army encamped in August 1781. *Library of Congress.*

146

frustrated at the lack of mounted troops and militia sent to his headquarters and still wary of Cornwallis, despite his adversary's inactivity. "The two sides pretend to be sleeping," he wrote to his cousin the Prince de Poix, a young French officer serving in the Continental Army, "but from a cursory glance I think they will soon awaken." Lafayette "would rather be rid of Cornwallis than a third of his army," he wrote to the Chevalier de La Luzerne, adding that although "we wage war like gentlemen...after all this, in the end he will give me a thrashing."[328]

In his letter from King William County to La Luzerne in mid-August, he wrote plaintively of the military situation he faced in Virginia. "If the French army could all of a sudden arrive in Virginia and be supported by a [naval] squadron," Lafayette opined, "we could do some very good things." Perhaps Lafayette would have been more confident in the course of events to come—and in avoiding a thrashing—had he known that his wishes were soon to be fulfilled.[329]

"BRAVERY, FORTITUDE, ZEAL AND DISCIPLINE"

The Conclusion of Lafayette's Campaign

Like the leaves of the forest when Summer is green,
That host with their banners at sunset were seen:
Like the leaves of the forest when Autumn has blown,
That host on the morrow lay withered and strown.
—Lord Byron, *"The Destruction of Sennacherib," 1815*

In May 1781, Admiral Jacques-Melchior de Barras de Saint-Laurent, Comte de Barras, and the General Donatien-Marie-Joseph de Vimeur, Vicomte de Rochambeau, arrived in Newport, Rhode Island, where French army and naval forces had made their headquarters since the previous year. These allied officers intended to cooperate in military operations with General Washington, acting under his orders. The Virginian had long sought to collaborate with the French against British forces in America, but he had been unsuccessful in bringing about successful joint operations. To coordinate the maneuvers of the combined forces, the French officers and the American commander met in Wethersfield, Connecticut, for three days beginning on May 21. Washington made clear his preference for an attack on British-occupied New York City, with Rochambeau moving many of his 5,300 infantrymen to Newburgh where Washington's 6,650 troops were encamped on the Hudson River, while the warships of de Barras would support the attack on New York City by sea. The American general considered the time ripe for taking the city, as Clinton had weakened his garrison there since December by sending troops to Virginia and the Carolinas. "I know of no measure," Washington concluded, "which will be so likely to afford relief to the southern states, in so short a time, as a serious menace against New York."[330]

Rochambeau, overall commander of the French expeditionary force, favored operations against the British in the Chesapeake over an attack against New York, in order to prevent the enemy's conquest of the South. However, Admiral de Barras opposed a Chesapeake foray due to current British naval superiority in American waters and a lack of transports available to bring French forces to Virginia. Washington concurred with de Barras, although he did not rule out a combined campaign in the Chesapeake if circumstances were favorable.[331]

There was one additional factor influencing Franco-American planning during the spring of 1781—a second French fleet under Admiral François-Joseph Paul de Grasse, Comte de Grasse, had sailed from Brest, France, in early April and was headed for the West Indies. How this fleet would fit in to operations in North America during 1781 was as yet unknown to the planners at Wethersfield. Attempting to overcome the objections of de Barras and Washington to waging war in the Chesapeake, Rochambeau wrote to de Grasse a few days after the Connecticut meeting, urging him to sail north from the Caribbean to Virginia. "The arrival of M. le Comte de Grasse may save the country," he stated, asking him to bring French soldiers as well. In mid-June, Rochambeau again wrote to de Grasse, imploring him to bring to the American coast "as many troops as possible" and hard money to pay for supplies. "These people are at the end of their means," he advised de Grasse, and the admiral was much needed there with his powerful flotilla to give the allies naval superiority.[332]

Rochambeau's 4,400 troops united with Washington's army on July 6 on the east bank of the Hudson at Dobbs Ferry, New York. Washington and Rochambeau reconnoitered Clinton's lines around New York City and eventually realized that the enemy was too strongly entrenched there to attack. This left the American commander "exceedingly anxious" and in a most "perplexing and ridiculous situation," wrote a Connecticut officer, "not being able to determine on any fixed plan of operation, from the incertainty of his expectations and prospects." Now without the realistic opportunity to take New York, Washington instead looked southward to his home state for a theater of operations in which to make full use of his French allies.[333]

Then, on August 14, Rochambeau received an electrifying message from de Grasse, written on July 28: the French admiral would sail on

The Thomas Nelson House (right) in Yorktown, the river port held by British troops beginning in August 1781. *Library of Congress.*

August 13 to the Chesapeake Bay from Santo Domingo with three thousand troops from that island's garrison, along with artillery and siege guns and money collected at Havana en route. Washington also received a copy of the important letter on the fourteenth, which noted that de Grasse would commit to this cooperative campaign only through October 15, since the troops he intended to bring were needed back in the West Indies later that month. "Make the best use of this precious time," de Grasse urged Rochambeau. No doubt Washington was excited at the prospects now before him, despite the time constraints under which he would have to work. With New York no longer a feasible objective for the combined forces, he was now given a second chance to deal the enemy a potentially crushing blow, this time far to the south. Washington wasted no time upon receipt of the favorable news. The first Continental troops began their long southward trek on August 17, followed two days later by the battalions of French soldiers, and from Newport, de Barras quickly set sail with his fleet for the Chesapeake Bay.[334]

Washington recognized that with two French fleets making for the Chesapeake, it was now crucial to his plans that Lafayette keep the British at Yorktown. He sent a courier on August 15 to the marquis to inform him that de Grasse would soon be in Virginia waters, and he should keep Wayne's troops in Virginia. Lafayette was to prevent Cornwallis's army from escaping into North Carolina as well. Receiving this news by August 21, Lafayette replied that he would move to the Chickahominy River and perhaps on to James Town with his 2,500 Continentals and 3,000 militiamen. Washington wrote again to Lafayette on August 21, reminding him that "the enemy on the arrival of the fleet should not have it in their power to effect their retreat" and that his troops and the French infantry were on their way from the Hudson. The marquis was elated not only that the year's primary campaign would be focused in Tidewater Virginia but also that his beloved commander would personally come to the Chesapeake Bay to lead the effort.[335]

Lafayette ordered Wayne to cross the James River at Westover to assume a position on the Southside, blocking the main roads to North Carolina. The marquis moved his own force on August 31 from his camps around Romancoke to the Pamunkey River, crossed at Ruffin's Ferry and then marched to Holt's Forge (now Providence Forge) on the Williamsburg Road in New Kent County, about twenty-five miles west of Williamsburg. By this time, he felt free to divulge to Governor Nelson "that such a force may be shortly expected from the West Indies, Rhode Island, and General Washington's army as will certainly (if properly supported) put an end to the war in this state and finally capture the invaders." He chided the governor about Virginia's failure to provide for his army and raise adequate militia, especially since the forces of France, America and Spain were then jointly operating to liberate the commonwealth. He still required dragoons; his men lacked shoes, arms and ammunition and were "living from hand to mouth." To support Wayne on the Southside, he sought to have six hundred militia posted there under General Lawson, but few turned out. Cornwallis was too dangerous a foe, Lafayette knew, to expect him to remain idle while American and French forces concentrated to ensnare him in the Chesapeake region.[336]

On August 30, de Grasse appeared in the lower Chesapeake Bay with twenty-eight ships and 3,250 well-equipped soldiers ready for duty and advised the marquis that day of his arrival. "From the bottom of my heart," Lafayette warmly wrote Washington the following day, "I congratulate you upon the arrival of the French fleet." He went on to report that "I am in a very charming situation, and find myself at the head of a beautiful body of troops." The French soldiers under the command of the Marquis de St. Simon, ordered to act under Lafayette's command, were shipped to James Island in dozens of boats and landed there on September 2, "which spread an universal joy among our officers and soldiers," wrote a Pennsylvania officer who watched the allies' landing from the south bank of the James.

The Governor's Palace in Williamsburg. *Library of Congress.*

Once the French regiments arrived to bolster the Patriot troops, Lafayette directed Wayne to move to Surrey County and cross to James Town Island on the third.[337] Lafayette brought his own troops eastward on the flat roads of the Peninsula, across Diascund Creek, past Chickahominy Church and Norrell's Mill and on to Green Spring Plantation on September 3 in a heavy rain. By the night of September 7, the marquis had joined the French and American forces and marched them to defensive positions at Williamsburg, about twelve miles from the enemy's location.[338]

As one of Lafayette's modern biographers observed, "This was La Fayette's last movement as an independent commander in America." With the French now in the Chesapeake; Washington, Rochambeau and de Barras on their way there; and Cornwallis's army dug in at Yorktown and Gloucester Point, the young French general in American service would now take a subordinate part in the final major campaign of the war, culminating in the British surrender on October 19 after a twenty-two-day siege along the York River. It was, as the marquis described it, a "glorious, and important success."[339]

Recalling his arduous Fabian maneuvers from Richmond to the Rapidan and then to Mechunk Creek and eventually down to the lower James, Lafayette reflected on the innumerable difficulties he and his soldiers had faced in Virginia from late April through early September. Against

Cornwallis, "it was not without difficulty that we avoided the battle he was seeking," he wrote to his wife in late August. "After many excursions we became stronger than we had been at first, and we pretended to be much stronger still. We regained what we had lost without risking a battle, and after two small skirmishes the enemy army returned to Portsmouth." Shortly after Cornwallis's capitulation, the marquis told a prominent Boston clergyman that "the storm that had been gathered against this small army gave us a great deal of trouble to maintain the vessel afloat," and "nothing but the bravery, fortitude zeal and discipline of our regular force, [and] the patriotism, and patience of our militia, could have saved us from ruin, and extricated us from our innumerable difficulties."[340] The American Congress in Philadelphia shared these sentiments and, in November 1781, passed a resolution praising him for his successful campaign in Virginia and "his judgment, vigilance, gallantry, and address in its defence." As a demonstration of its esteem for him, Congress voted to reimburse the marquis the £2,000 he spent of his own funds at Alexandria for the relief of his ragged soldiers.[341]

Perhaps Governor Thomas Nelson's assessment of the marquis is the most accurate, as he had ample opportunity to observe him in 1781. "You could not have made the Virginians more happy in a Commander than in the Marquis," he wrote to George Washington that summer. "They have great confidence in his bravery & Conduct. His regard for the Civil rights of the People, and His attention to the preservation of their property is very pleasing to them. In short his Character is held in the highest estimation by them."[342]

"A CATALOGUE OF OMISSIONS AND OTHER MISCONDUCT"

Ingratitude is the most abominable of sins.
—Saint Ignatius, sixteenth century

On August 7, 1781, Thomas Jefferson received a letter at Monticello from John Beckley, clerk of the Virginia House of Delegates. Writing at the request of the House on June 12 from Staunton, where the assembly had relocated after Tarleton's Charlottesville raid, Beckley sent him "information respecting a Resolution of their House, of this Date, for an Enquirey into the Conduct of the Executive for the last twelve Months." The inquiry was to be made at the next session of the Assembly, set for October. Also on June 12, Thomas Nelson Jr. was elected to a one-year term as governor.[343]

Beckely's official letter to Jefferson was not the first the former governor had heard of an examination into his conduct while he had served as the state's chief executive. On June 19, the president of the Senate, Archibald Cary, had written from Staunton to advise him that his nephew, George Nicholas of Albemarle County, "made a Motion in the Delegates House for an Inquire into your Conduct," which Cary called "a Catalogue of omissions, and other Misconduct."[344]

Those who supported the call for an investigation were frustrated at the state government's ineffective handling of the demands of war once Virginia began to suffer repeated invasions and as government authorities became more heavy-handed in impressing horses, frequently drafting men during times of need on their farms and failing to repel the British. Jefferson, state officials and Continental officers worked tirelessly to create an effective defense for their commonwealth and to support Continental forces under Lafayette, Greene and von Steuben, but the state simply did not have the organizational structure to manufacture, collect or transport military materiel to the proper locations in adequate quantity. "No state abounding with such a plenty as Virginia, ever experienced such a scarcity for want of order and a proper application of her supplies," wrote General Greene, who had as much experience working with Virginia authorities as any general during the war.[345] Lafayette sympathized with Jefferson's predicament and instead blamed the structure of the state government. "The Wheels of [Virginia's] Government are so very rusty that no Governor whatever will be able to set them fiercely agoing," he wrote in September, adding that "time will prove that Jefferson has been too severely charged."[346]

Before receiving a copy of the House resolution, an obviously aggrieved Jefferson wrote curtly to Nicholas from Monticello on July 28.

> *I am informed that a resolution on your motion passed the House of Delegates requiring me to render account of some part of my administration without specifying the act to be accounted for. As I suppose that this was done under the impression of some particular instance or instances of ill conduct, and that it could not be intended just to stab a reputation by a general suggestion under a bare expectation that facts might be afterwards hunted up to boulster it, I hope you will not think me improper in asking the favor of you to specify to me the unfortunate passages in my conduct which you mean to adduce against me, that I may be enabled to prepare to yield obedience to the house while facts are fresh in my memory and witnesses and documents are in existence.*[347]

As the editors of *The Papers of Thomas Jefferson* point out, the term "executive" used in the June 12 resolution may have referred to the governor *and* his council. It is plain, however, in Jefferson's language in the letter to Nicholas that he understood the inquiry was to be directed primarily at himself by his political enemies.[348]

Jefferson was stung by the criticism and decided to dispute the implied accusations despite having "retired to my farm, my family and books from which I think nothing will ever more separate me." However, "a desire to leave public office with a reputation not more blotted than it has deserved will oblige me to emerge at the next session of our assembly and perhaps to accept of a seat in it, but as I go with a single object, I shall withdraw when that shall be accomplished." He felt that despite his best efforts while in office, "these…have not been such to give satisfaction to some of my countrymen" and that he had to show the public that "suggestion and fact are different things."[349]

Nicholas soon replied to Jefferson's letter. He told the former governor defensively that he was not "an accuser" and had "no private pique to gratify." Rather, "as a freeman and the representative of free Men I considered it as both my right and duty to call upon the executive to account for our numberless miscarriages and losses so far as they were concerned in or might have prevented them." He assured Jefferson that "if (as I hope it may) it shall appear that they [the Council and Jefferson] have done everything in their power to prevent our misfortunes I will most readily retract any opinion that I may have formed to their prejudice." He went on to list several matters he wished to see addressed by the upcoming legislative inquiry, including "the total want of opposition to Arnold on his first expedition to Richmond," the "great loss that the country has sustained in arms &c. exclusive of those destroyed by the enemy" and instances of what he considered as mishandling of the militia by the executive in 1781.[350]

In late November, the House of Delegates meeting in Richmond appointed a committee—which included George Nicholas—to receive any charges against the state executive and draw up charges for the inquiry. At his own request, Jefferson was appointed a delegate to the assembly from Albemarle and took his seat in December, at which opportunity he answered the charges against him made by Nicholas in his July 31 letter—although Nicholas was not present at the session. No other accusations or complaints were lodged by any members. By this time, with the American victory at Yorktown fresh in their minds, the summer's enthusiasm for the controversial inquiry had evaporated so that the legislature dropped the matter. On December 12, the delegates officially gave Jefferson their unanimous "sincere thanks" for his "impartial, upright, and attentive administration whilst in office" in order to "obviate and remove all unmerited censure." In a further mark of confidence in Jefferson by Virginia's delegates, they elected him the same day to serve in Congress, although he declined the office.[351] Still, Jefferson was dogged for his wartime gubernatorial administration for years by his political opponents, who chose to blame him for the results of the destructive British raids.[352]

While most of Virginia's leaders must have known that Jefferson was not individually responsible for the state's ineffective response to British incursions into the commonwealth from 1779 to 1781, the master of Monticello did receive criticism for his actions at the expiration of his second gubernatorial term. As noted, Jefferson's term was set to expire on June 2, and after many trials and burdens as chief executive, he looked forward to "that period of relief which the Constitution has prepared for those oppressed with the labours of my office, and a long declared resolution of relinquishing it to abler hands has prepared my way for retirement to a private station." Although the legislature set June 4 for the election of his successor and Jefferson remained in Charlottesville through part of that day while the delegates were in town, he seems to have regarded himself as free from the burdens of office as of June 2, even though the election did not take place. Moreover, he did not follow the assembly to Staunton after Tarleton's raid but, instead, went to Poplar Forest, leaving the state with no chief executive. It should also be recalled that the state's lieutenant governor, Dudley Digges, had already resigned his office, so the governorship could not fall upon him. Years later, Jefferson wrote that he suggested General Nelson be elected governor to unite "the civil and military power in the same hands at this time" and "greatly facilitate military measures."[353]

With British troops moving across central Virginia with impunity and the state legislature scattered by enemy dragoons, Jefferson's decision to retire to Bedford rankled some Virginians and had the appearance of abandoning the ship of state in a dangerous storm. His successor, Nelson, was not elected until June 12, which led Richard Henry Lee to complain to General Washington that "we remain without government at a time when the most wise and most vigorous administration of the public affairs can also save us from the ruin determined for us by the enemy."[354] To Virginia's congressional delegation, Lee reported that "Mr. Jefferson had resigned his office & retired," and that "without either executive or Legislative authority, every thing [is] in the greatest possible confusion."[355] Stories began to circulate soon after Tarleton's soldiers left Charlottesville that Jefferson had ingloriously fled town and that his conduct was laughable. A Southside militia colonel wrote on June 9 that without a proper government in Virginia, "I… cannot bear to see her neglected," and one of the council members told Jefferson that he heard "daily complaints and reproaches of the people" aimed at the executive, though the anger may have been directed more at the council than the governor.[356]

In the postwar years, Jefferson's political detractors, such as a South Carolinian who stated that he abandoned "his office and his trust, at the most critical moment," used the events surrounding Tarleton's unwelcome visit to Charlottesville to smear him, even with a hint of cowardice. Some later historians (though certainly not most) adopted this perspective as well, such as Bryan Conrad, who, in a 1934 academic article, wrote that Jefferson "was invincible in peace and invisible in war."[357]

These accusations rankled the future president for years, particularly during the national elections of 1796 and 1800, despite his many public and private accomplishments for which he was justifiably famous. Jefferson called them "nonsense," and in his own words—prepared for publication—described his incredulity at being indicted by public opinion for years "through the slanderous chronicles" of the Federalist Party.

> *Would it be believed…that this flight from a troop of horse, whose whole legion, too, was within supporting distance, has been the subject, with party writers, of volumes of reproach on me, serious or sarcastic? That it has been sung in verse, and said in humble prose, that…I declined a combat singly against a troop, in which victory would have been so glorious?*[358]

In fact, Jefferson took pains to point out that George Nicholas, the delegate who first raised a question about Jefferson's wartime conduct while governor, "took a conspicuous occasion afterwards, of his own free will, and when the matter was entirely at rest, to retract publicly the erroneous opinions he had been led into on that occasion, and to make just reparation by a candid acknowledgment of them."[359]

Appendix

SITES OF THE 1781 VIRGINIA CAMPAIGN

Many of the sites associated with the 1781 Virginia campaign of Lafayette and Cornwallis can be seen today, even though most are privately owned or, in the case of structures, no longer standing. The roads over which the belligerents traveled across the state's Piedmont and Tidewater regions can still be followed. Although modern development has intruded into some of the Old Dominion's terrain where the armies marched, skirmished and camped, much of the rural nature of the 1781 "seat of war" remains today. Readers will find below several descriptions of how to follow the paths of the American and British forces in central Virginia and find the locations of the relevant fords, bridges, plantations, churches, crossroads, skirmishes and encampments. While the descriptions have been arranged so as to follow the routes of the key leaders involved in the campaign, several overlap or are close enough to each other to follow simultaneously.

CORNWALLIS'S MARCH THROUGH CENTRAL VIRGINIA

General Cornwallis and his army entered Virginia in May 1781, having marched north from Halifax, North Carolina. His troops crossed the Meherrin River at Hick's Ford, now Emporia. Marching north, Cornwallis's column was met by Simcoe's rangers south of the Nottoway near Stony Creek, then proceeded to Petersburg following the Halifax Road, modern

Route 618, then 604. Cornwallis then moved east on May 24 to Maycox, the site of which is now within the James River National Wildlife Refuge on the south bank of the river. Here his army, combined with Phillips's troops, crossed the James to Westover, located two miles south of Route 5 (John Tyler Highway) on Route 633 (Westover Road) in Charles City County.

From Westover, the British marched west along modern Route 5 to Turkey Island Creek and then turned north on Willis Church Road/Elko Road (Route 156, past the 1862 Malvern Hill battlefield site and Glendale National Cemetery), to White Oak Swamp. The site of their encampment here is unknown, but the troops next likely turned right off Elko Road north of the swamp onto White Oak Road and then to Bottoms Bridge, on U.S. Route 60 (Williamsburg Road) at the Chickahominy River. Following several small roads and lanes north from the bridge, Cornwallis brought his army to Newcastle on the Pamunkey River. The site of this town, now gone, was located about a mile downstream from the U.S. Route 360 (Mechanicsville Turnpike) bridge over the Pamunkey.

Next, the British proceeded north to Hanovertown by way of Route 605 (River Road). Now disappeared, this port was situated at the bend of Route 605 north of Hanover Town Road (Route 604). Cornwallis then pushed on along Route 605 to modern U.S. Route 301, turned north and reached Hanover Court House. Here the original eighteenth-century courthouse is still in use. The British force soon advanced to the North Anna River by way of Route 646 (Hickory Hill Road) and Route 738 (Old Ridge Road) across the South Anna River. The army encamped at Cook's Ford, located north of modern Route 684 (Verdon Road) about one mile west of the modern U.S. Route 1 bridge and within the North Anna Battlefield Park.

After Tarleton and Simcoe left this camp to raid Charlottesville and Point of Fork, Cornwallis marched west on Verdon Road and then south on Routes 738 (Teman Road) and 735 (Annfield Road), which used to cross the Newfound River but no longer continues. On the opposite side of the river, the British Route continues on Routes 740 (Chiswell Lane) and 685 (Scotchtown Road) to Scotchtown, Patrick Henry's former home. (It is also possible that the army crossed the Newfound River farther west, along Route 738, Coatesville Road.)

Cornwallis's route can next be followed from Scotchtown by continuing south on Route 685 (Scotchtown Road) to Route 671 at Ebenezer Baptist Church, then going five miles farther south to U.S. Route 33 (Mountain Road). The redcoats turned east here to cross the South Anna at Ground Squirrel Bridge and then marched right in one mile onto modern Route 670

(Stone Horse Creek Road) to encamp around "Mount Brilliant," two and one half miles farther on the right side of the road. On June 5, probably by way of Rockville and Route 620 (Dogwood Trail Road), Cornwallis proceeded south about twelve miles to Napier's Mill, situated on Horsepen Creek in Goochland County behind the current post office building at present-day Oilville, just south of U.S. 250 (Broad Street Road). The British marched west from the mill on what is now Route 632 (Fairgrounds Road) to the Bates Plantation, located along Cheney's Creek on the north side of Route 6 just west of Goochland County High School.

Following Route 6 (the River Road) west, the British advanced to Jefferson's Elk-hill farm, which was situated south of Route 6 on Route 608 (Elk Hill Road). The large white house seen on the hilltop on the east side of 608 is a nineteenth-century structure; the eighteenth-century house, no longer standing, was on the treeless hill above the modern railroad on the west side of the road.

Tarleton's Charlottesville Raid

Tarleton left Cook's Ford on June 3 and rode west on Route 684 (Verdon Road) to Brown's Ordinary in western Hanover County, where it meets Route 738. His column passed Scotchtown no doubt using the same route Cornwallis did two days later. After reaching Ground Squirrel Bridge on Mountain Road (U.S. 33), his troopers rode west to Cuckoo Tavern, which stood where Mountain Road intersects with U.S. 522. Although the tavern no longer exists, a marker there indicates its former site. Tarleton's cavalry continued west on Mountain Road; then it went through Louisa Court House and rested nearby. The dragoons next advanced west along Route 22 (Louisa Road) to Boswell's Tavern, which still stands on the north side of the road just east of the intersection with U.S. 15 (James Madison Highway). After they burned a dozen wagons here, they proceeded farther west, probably turning right off Route 22 onto Lindsay Road (Routes 675 and 615) to raid several plantations, including Castle Hill and Belvoir, along today's Louisa Road (Route 22) and Gordonsville Road (Route 231). These farms are privately owned today and are not visible from the roadway.

Tarleton moved on to Charlottesville by riding south on Louisa Road and then turned west on the Three Notch'd Road (near Shadwell), which is for the most part modern U.S. Route 250. His dragoons rode into Charlottesville by crossing the Rivanna River at Secretary's Ford, located near the east end of East Market Street north of the modern I-64 bridge and visible from the Old Mills Trail (on the east bank of the river). Tarleton encamped at the Farm, which is located west of the Rivanna River at Jefferson and Twelfth Streets Northeast, now in the city. The building used as his headquarters is the white brick structure still standing on the property, which is privately owned.

Jack Jouett's Ride

It is uncertain which road Jouett followed to Charlottesville to warn Jefferson of Tarleton's approach, but it seems likely that from Cuckoo Tavern, he followed today's Route 640 (Jack Jouett Road), between U.S. Route 33 and the Three Chopt Road (U.S. Route 250). At some point, he came into the Three Chopt Road and then crossed the Rivanna at Milton on Route 729, downriver from Secretary's Ford, before riding four more miles west to Monticello on modern Route 732 and Route 53 (Thomas Jefferson Parkway).

Jefferson's Escape Route

Leaving Monticello, Jefferson most likely traveled south to Enniscorthy on Route 53 and then went right (south) on modern Route 795, which continues south as Route 627 (Carters Mountain Road). He arrived at Enniscorthy, a half mile to the south of Route 712 (Plank Road). The family then went south by an uncertain route (probably by way of Esmont) to Joplin's Ordinary at a ford on the Rockfish River, where the present bridge on Route 722 (Rockfish Crossing Road) crosses that river. From this crossing the Jeffersons' path continued along Route 722 and then west through Findlay's Gap on Route 647, near Shipman, fourteen miles south. The Jefferson family's route from this gap to Hughes's plantation (Geddes) is unknown. Hughes's former home (privately owned) is on Route 700 near modern Clifford, south of the Tye River and west of U.S. Route 29 in northern Amherst County.

SIMCOE'S ROUTE TO POINT OF FORK

From Cook's Ford, Simcoe moved south across Hanover County to Three Chopt Road in Goochland County and probably rode west to Byrd's Ordinary on the north side of the crossroads of U.S. Route 250 and Route 626, two and a half miles west of modern Ferncliff in Louisa County. From here, he likely followed a road southward along the east bank of the Rivanna, which he crossed at Napier's Ford, located south of modern Palmyra. To reach Point of Fork, he likely traveled south along a road now covered by U.S. 15 to the River Road (Route 6) at today's hamlet called Dixie. From here, his troops rode about four miles east to Point of Fork, turning right off the River Road along what is now Route 624 west of Columbia. Little remains of the arsenal buildings, and the location is on private property.

LAFAYETTE'S MARCHES FROM RICHMOND TO MECHUNK CREEK

Once Cornwallis crossed the James at Westover, Lafayette sought to avoid the enemy by marching to the west and north of Cornwallis. From Richmond, his route took his troops north to Brook's Bridge, where U.S. Route 1 crosses Upham Brook, two-tenths of a mile south of Hilliard Road in the Lakeside area of Henrico County. Crossing the Chickahominy River into Hanover County at or near Winston's Bridge, a half mile south of Sliding Hill Road, Lafayette continued northwest, probably along Routes 623 (Cedar Lane) to Rockville on Route 271 (Pouncey Tract Road). He soon reached Dandridge's plantation in western Hanover County on Route 611 (Vontay Road), one-tenth of a mile east of Route 617 (Pinhook Road). The house, Oldfield, still stands and is privately owned. Lafayette's troops then moved north across the South Anna at Ground Squirrel Bridge, camped at Scotchtown and marched to the North Anna River at Anderson's Bridge, on Route 658 (Tyler Station Road and Green Bay Road), three miles south of modern Partlow. Rather than crossing here, however, the marquis' men crossed the North Anna River at Davenport's Ford, located downstream at the modern bridge on Route 738 (Anderson Mill Road), about two and a half miles north of Beaverdam.

Lafayette's small force then advanced to Mattaponi Church, although his precise route from Davenport's Ford to this now disappeared chapel is unknown. It is likely the American column went north along today's Partlow Road (Route 738) and crossed the Ta River, just north of the Spotsylvania County community called Blades Corner. The location of the church was on the hilltop on the east side of the road just north of the Ta River, south of Locklear Landing Drive.

After camping at Mattaponi Church, Lafayette and his troops went to Corbin's Bridge on the Po River along modern Route 612 (Catharpin Road), west of today's Todd's Tavern. After the soldiers crossed this span, they marched northeast on Catharpin Road to Todd's Tavern and then north on Route 613 (Brock Road) to halt at the bridge over Wilderness Run, located on Route 3 (Plank Road) one-tenth of a mile from its intersection with Route 20 (Constitution Highway). Their encampment was on the east side of the stream south of Route 3 and can be viewed from the small National Park Service parking area at the Wilderness Tavern site.

From Wilderness Run, Lafayette marched his men north by an unknown route to Ely's Ford, located where modern Route 610 (Ely's Ford Road) crosses the Rapidan River. The soldiers then turned west on Ely's Ford Road and marched ten miles to the site of the Lower or Great Fork Church, which Lafayette called "Culpeper Church." This structure was on the north side of Route 610, at this point named Madden's Tavern Road, fewer than three-tenths of a mile east of Route 724 (Youngs Lane) and one and a half miles north of Lignum, but it has disappeared.

Lafayette moved his men along the north bank of the Rapidan along Route 647 (Algonquin Trail) to Raccoon Ford, accessible by turning south (left) on Route 617 (Raccoon Ford Road). There is no bridge here at the Rapidan, so to continue the marquis' line of march, one must restart the route on the opposite side of the river in Orange County on Raccoon Ford Road, there designated Route 611. The American troops traveled south from Raccoon Ford to the neighborhood of Rhoadesville, ten miles away on the north side of Route 20. Continuing his southward trek, Lafayette—having been joined by Wayne's troops somewhere in this section—proceeded to Brock's Bridge on the North Anna River, twelve miles south. His route to this spot is unknown, but Lafayette probably led his men from Rhoadesville west to modern Unionville on Route 671 and then south on Route 669, later called Marquis Road. From this bridge, the rebel army went south to Boswell's Tavern in Louisa County, having crossed the South Anna River a mile to the north on U.S Route 15.

The disused road Lafayette's men cleared to move from Boswell's Tavern to Mechunk Creek is not known today. At Mechunk Creek, the American troops were posted on the high ground on the west side of this stream on the Three Notch'd/Chopt Road, which in this section is Route 759. The bridge Lafayette's men overlooked on Route 759 was four-tenths of a mile north of U.S. 250 and two miles east of the Boyd Tavern Exit (129) of Interstate 64. The site of Allegre's Tavern, part of which is extant, is also west of the bridge on the hill east of the road.

THE ARMIES MOVE TO RICHMOND

Retiring to Richmond, Cornwallis's army utilized the River Road, today's Route 6. The redcoats camped along the way at Goochland Court House, Dover Creek Church (about ten miles to the east at Sabot) and Tuckahoe Plantation, before halting again at Westham. (Note that when traveling east on Route 6, River Road turns southeast/right onto Route 650 seven-tenths of a mile east of Route 623, Hockett Road.) Simcoe followed the main army as a rear guard while Tarleton's dragoons moved east along the Three Chopt Road from Byrd's Tavern. His cavalrymen rode past Peer's Tavern, located in modern Centerville one-tenth of a mile north of Broad Street Road (U.S. 250) on the west side of Route 708, St. Matthews Lane.

It is not known precisely which roads Lafayette used to follow the British, although it seems clear he marched north of the Three Chopt Road to Dandridge's Plantation in western Hanover. He may have used part of the road Jouett employed on his ride to Monticello and certainly stayed south of the South Anna River. He is known to have crossed Deep Creek in Louisa County, which he possibly managed on Route 640, there called East Old Mountain Road, about one mile west of U.S. Route 522. The American forces likely proceeded east along the right bank of the South Anna River following U.S. 522 south and then veered left/east onto Route 663 (Owens Creek Road) to cross Owens Creek. It is possible that Lafayette turned left off Route 663 and proceeded onto Route 611 (Octagon Church Road), which eventually reached Dandridge's home near Vontay.

From Dandridge's, the marquis attempted to attack Tarleton north of Richmond near Meadow Bridge, which is located on the Chickahominy River on today's Meadowbridge Road (Route 627) about two miles from the Richmond International Raceway. Soon thereafter, he marched his command to Richmond, halting on the way at Prosser's Plantation on North Run in the approximate area of Lakeside Country Club and the Parham

Road campus of J. Sargeant Reynolds Community College. Cornwallis left Richmond on June 20 and marched to Williamsburg by way of Bottoms Bridge on U.S. Route 60 and New Kent Court House on today's Route 249, followed by the marquis' forces along these and other routes.

WAYNE'S MARCH TO JOIN LAFAYETTE

Although rarely described in histories of the 1781 Virginia campaign or in biographies of Wayne, the Pennsylvanians' march from York to Lafayette's army in Virginia is well documented and easy to follow on modern roads, thanks largely to Wayne's letters and the journals of several of his officers.

Beginning on May 26, Wayne's brigade marched from York, Pennsylvania, to Frederick, Maryland, and then reached the north bank of the Potomac River. The troops crossed this river at Noland's Ferry, about four miles east of the U.S. Route 15 bridge at Point of Rocks, Maryland, and accessible by Nolands Ferry Road from Tuscarora, Maryland. Once in Virginia, Wayne's route was through today's Lucketts and Leesburg and then south on the Carolina Road, which is approximated today by U.S. Route 15 (James Monroe Highway). He crossed Goose Creek at Cox's Mill in the area of Oatlands Plantation and then went on to the Red House in modern Haymarket at the junction of Thoroughfare Gap Road (Route 55) and the Carolina Road in Prince William County. Wayne's route south on the Carolina Road from Haymarket is now obscured by U.S. Route 29, Lake Manassas and several golf courses, but it can be picked up again south of the lake at Greenwich at the intersection of Vint Hill Road (Route 215) and Greenwich Road (Route 603). Moving south on Greenwich Road, Wayne's troops turned west on the Dumfries Road (Route 605) and then south on Route 670 to Auburn, then called Neavil's Ordinary. Here, they forded Cedar Run where the modern bridge is today and then continued south along Rougue's Road (Route 602) to Turkey Run, where the army camped one night.

From here, Wayne advanced by way of present-day Cassanova, continuing on Rougue's Road (Route 602) to the settlement of Germantown, most of which has since disappeared, and a large public lake at Crockett Park now blocks the original course of the road. Route 602 continues south of the lake, and Wayne followed it to Midland, where his men continued marching east on Route 610, crossing Catlett Road (Route 28) and arriving at the intersection with Route 806, Elk Run Church Road. A small visitors' center here with limited hours and some outdoor signage interprets the old Elk Run Anglican Church, now vanished.

Wayne proceeded southwest from here by an uncertain path to Norman's Ford on the Rappahannock at the west end of Route 654, near present-day Remington, three miles away. From this ford, his men trudged south and rested one night at or near modern Stevensburg at the junction of Route 3 and Route 663, six miles east of Culpeper. Moving south from Stevensburg, Wayne cross the Rapidan River at Raccoon Ford and then proceeded to follow Lafayette until the two commands united on June 10.

THE END OF THE CAMPAIGN

The skirmish at Spencer's Ordinary was fought along today's Centerville Road (Route 614) northwest of Williamsburg in James City County. The initial British line was along Longhill Road (Route 612), and much of the fighting took place in what is now Freedom Park. Lafayette's main encampment at the time of the battle was at Chickahominy Church, near Little Creek Reservoir at the intersection of Cranston's Mill Pond, Chickahominy and Little Creek Dam Roads. Some troops were also posted at Norrell's Mill, located on Cranston's Mill Pond Road at Yarmouth Creek.

The Battle of Green Spring was fought in the area around the modern Jamestown Settlement, administered by the Commonwealth of Virginia. Wayne's troops approached the British position by way of Greenspring Road (Route 614), and much of the action was along today's Route 31.

NOTES

Chapter 1

1. Charles Cornwallis to Henry Clinton, April 10, 1781, Clark, *State Records of North Carolina*, 17:1,010–12 (hereafter cited as *NCSR*).
2. "Return of Charles Cornwallis's Brigade of the British Army 1781," *NCSR*, 17:1,009; Cornwallis to Clinton, April 10, 1781, *NCSR*, 17:1,010–12; Morrissey, *Yorktown 1781*, 16–17.
3. Cornwallis to Clinton, April 10, 1781, *NCSR*, 17:1,010–12.
4. For an overview of Cornwallis's life and early service in the American Revolution, see Wickwire and Wickwire, *Cornwallis*; Marquis de Lafayette to the Chevalier de La Luzerne, August 14, 1781, Idzerda, *Lafayette in the Age of the American Revolution*, 4:321–22.
5. Willcox, "British Road to Yorktown."
6. Cornwallis to Clinton, April 10, 1781, *NCSR*, 17:1,010–12.
7. Cornwallis to George Germain, April 18, 1781, *NCSR*, 17:1,015–16.
8. Cornwallis to Clinton, April 23, 1781, *NCSR*, 17:1,018–19; Cornwallis to Germain, April 23, 1781, *NCSR*, 17:1,016–18.
9. William Phillips to Henry Clinton, March 29–30, 1781, Saberton, *Cornwallis Papers*, 5:15–16.
10. Cornwallis to Phillips, April 24, 1781, *NCSR*, 17:1,019–20; Cornwallis to Germain, April 23, 1781, *NCSR* 17:1,016–18.
11. Wickwire and Wickwire, *Cornwallis*, 319.
12. Cornwallis to Phillips, April 24, 1781, *NCSR*, 17:1,019–20.
13. Clinton to Cornwallis, April 13, 1781, *NCSR*, 17:1,013–14.

14. Clinton to Phillips, April 26, 1781, *NCSR*, 17:1,020–23; Willcox, "Road to Yorktown," 11–12.
15. Clinton to Cornwallis, April 30, 1781, *NCSR*, 17:1,023–26; "Return of Charles Cornwallis, Marquis Cornwallis' Brigade of the British Army," May 1781, *NCSR*, 17:1,027; O'Shaughnessy, *Men Who Lost America*, 238–44; Henry Clinton to Charles Cornwallis, May 29, 1781, *NCSR*, 17:1,035–37; Willcox, "Road to Yorktown," 120.
16. "Return of Cornwallis' Brigade," May 1781, *NCSR*, 17:1,027.
17. Cornwallis to Clinton, May 20, 1781, *NCSR*, 17:1,029–30; Morrissey, *Yorktown 1781*, 37; Faden, "Marches of Lord Cornwallis" 1787 map; Tarleton, *Campaigns*, 290; Benedict Arnold to Cornwallis, May 12, 1781, Saberton, *Cornwallis Papers*, 4:152.
18. Davis, *Where a Man Can Go*, 180–81; Tarleton, *Campaigns*, 290; Cornwallis to Lord Rawdon, May 20, 1781, Ross, *Correspondence of Cornwallis*, 1:99; Arnold to Cornwallis, May 16, 1781, Saberton, *Cornwallis Papers*, 4:15.
19. Davis, *Where a Man Can Go*, 131.
20. Cornwallis to Clinton, May 20, 1781, Ross, *Correspondence of Cornwallis*, 1:100; Carrington, *Battles*, 589; Saberton, *Cornwallis Papers*, 5:3.

CHAPTER 2

21. Selby, *Revolution in Virginia*, 204–5; Kimball, *Jefferson*, 53–55; Morrissey, *Yorktown 1781*, 14; McDonnell, *Politics of War*, 343–44.
22. Selby, *Revolution in Virginia*, 207–8; Kimball, *Jefferson*, 54.
23. Ward and Greer, *Richmond*, 71.
24. Gruber, *John Peebles' American War*, 340, 379, 390; Ward and Greer, *Richmond*, 71.
25. Ferling, *Jefferson and Hamilton*, 95–96.
26. Lee, *Patriot Above Profit*, 390.
27. Selby, *Revolution in Virginia*, 216–18; Kimball, *Jefferson*, 110–13; Ward and Greer, *Richmond*, 71–73; Lee, *Patriot Above Profit*, 390–92.
28. Selby, *Revolution in Virginia*, 220–21; Kimball, *Jefferson*, 114–17; Ward and Greer, *Richmond*, 73.
29. Ward and Greer, *Richmond*, 73–74; Morrissey, *Yorktown 1781*, 95; Benedict Arnold to Henry Clinton, January 21, 1781, Davies, *Documents of the American Revolution*; Lynch, "Grading British General Benedict Arnold."
30. Selby, *Revolution in Virginia*, 222–23; Kimball, *Jefferson*, 125; George Washington to Thomas Jefferson, January 2, 1781, Fitzpatrick, *Writings of Washington*, 21:51; Jefferson to Samuel Huntington, January 10, 1781, Thomas Jefferson Papers, LOC.

31. Lee, *Patriot Above Profit*, 397; "Arnold's Invasion, 1781," 131–32. The Westham arsenal was located along the James near today's University of Richmond campus.

32. Ward and Greer, *Richmond*, 73–78; Arnold to Clinton, May 12, 1781, "Arnold's Expedition to Richmond," 187–90; Jefferson to Huntington, January 10, 1781, Thomas Jefferson Papers, LOC.

33. Selby, *Revolution in Virginia*, 223–24; Kimball, *Jefferson*, 128–40, 144, 175; Ward and Greer, *Richmond*, 37–40, 74–75, 81.

34. Kimball, *Jefferson*, 141.

35. Morrissey, *Yorktown 1781*, 15, 96; Davis, *Where a Man Can Go*, 126.

36. Davis, *Where a Man Can Go*, 131; Clinton to Phillips, March 10, 1781, Saberton, *Cornwallis Papers*, 5:8.

37. Captain W. Thomas to Thomas Symonds, March 20, 1781, Palmer, *Calendar of State Papers*, 1:583.

38. Lafayette to General Washington, April 23, 1781, Idzerda, *Lafayette*, 4:60–61.

39. Lafayette, *Memoirs*, 1:408.

40. George Washington to Lund Washington, April 30, 1781, Fitzpatrick, *Writings of Washington*, 22:14–15.

41. Leslie to Cornwallis, June 3, 1781, Saberton, *Cornwallis Papers*, 5:164.

42. Morrissey, *Yorktown 1781*, 15; Davis, *Where a Man Can Go*, 126, 129, 132, 140; Tower, *La Fayette*, 2:291; Arnold to Clinton, May 12, 1781, "Arnold's Expedition to Richmond," *William and Mary Quarterly*, 187–90. Diascund Bridge was located near modern Lanexa.

43. Davis, *Where a Man Can Go*, 140–41; Lee, *Patriot Above Profit*, 415.

44. Kimball, *Jefferson*, 199–200; Davis, *Where a Man Can Go*, 141.

45. Davis, *Where a Man Can Go*, 142–43; Baron von Steuben to Nathanael Greene, April 25, 1781, Conrad, *Papers of Greene*, 8:147–48.

46. Davis, *Where a Man Can Go*, 133.

47. Morrissey, *Yorktown 1781*, 15; Davis, *Where a Man Can Go*, 144–46; von Steuben to Greene, April 25, 1781, Conrad, *Papers of Greene*, 8:147–48.

48. Davis, *Where a Man Can Go*, 151–52. Von Steuben's position west of Lieutenant Run was on today's Madison Street.

49. Von Steuben to Greene, April 25, 1781, Conrad, *Papers of Greene*, 8:147–48. Simcoe moved along what is today Graham Road.

50. Davis, *Where a Man Can Go*, 158–61, 165–66; Kimball, *Jefferson*, 214; von Steuben to Greene, April 25, 1781, Conrad, *Papers of Greene*, 8:147–48; Jefferson to von Steuben, April 26, 1781, Boyd, *Papers of Thomas Jefferson*, 5:559; Jefferson to Washington, May 9, 1781, Founders Online. The British artillery fired from what is now South Little Church Street.

51. Kimball, *Jefferson*, 214; Davis, *Where a Man Can Go*, 158–61, 165–66.

52. Tower, *La Fayette*, 2:293.

53. Arnold to Clinton, May 12, 1781, "Arnold's Expedition to Richmond," 187–90; Nelson, *Washington's Great Gamble*, 147–51.
54. Jefferson to Washington, May 9, 1781, Founders Online; Arnold to Clinton, May 12, 1781, "Arnold's Expedition to Richmond," 187–90.
55. Arnold to Clinton, May 12, 1781, "Arnold's Expedition to Richmond, 1781," 187–90; "Jefferson to Washington, 9 May 1781," Founders Online.
56. Morrissey, *Yorktown 1781*, 15–16; Davis, *Where a Man Can Go*, 168–69, 171–72, 177–79; Ward and Greer, *Richmond*, 88–89; Carrington, *Battles*, 591; Phillips to Cornwallis, May 6, 1781, Saberton, *Cornwallis Papers*, 5:69; Tower, *La Fayette*, 2:296; Arnold to Clinton, May 12, 1781, "Arnold's Expedition to Richmond," 187–90; Voorhis, "Bollingbrook."

Chapter 3

57. Bell, *Commanding Generals*, 52–53.
58. Wright, *Continental Army*, 163.
59. Ibid., 140–42, 163; Coakley and Conn, *War of the American Revolution*, 63–64.
60. Wright, *Continental Army*, 164–65; Clary and Whitehorne, *Inspectors General*, 33–56.
61. George Washington to John Hancock, 31 May 1777, Chase, *Papers of George Washington*, 9:593.
62. Circular to the States, October 18, 1780, Fitzpatrick, *Writings of Washington*, 20:209–10; Weigley, *Towards an American Army*, 1–11; Weigley, *American Way of War*, 3–17.
63. Washington quoted in Pancake, *This Destructive War*, 52.
64. Wright, "Corps of Light Infantry."
65. Wright, *Continental Army*, 149, 151, 167; Wright, "Corps of Light Infantry."
66. Washington to William Heath, February 15, 1781, Fitzpatrick, *Writings of Washington*, 21:228; Washington to Timothy Pickering, February 15, 1781, Fitzpatrick, *Writings of Washington*, 21:229.
67. Washington to Comte de Rochambeau, February 15, 1781, Fitzpatrick, *Writings of Washington*, 21:229–32.
68. Tower, *La Fayette*, 2:221–22.
69. Nelson, *Washington's Great Gamble*, 32–40; Virginia Delegates in Congress to Thomas Jefferson, February 1781, Hutchinson and Rachal, *Papers of James Madison*, 2:314–17; Tower, *La Fayette*, 2:223–25.
70. Washington to Lafayette, February 20, 1781, Fitzpatrick, *Writings of Washington*, 21:253.
71. Washington, "Instructions to Marquis de Lafayette," February 20, 1781, Fitzpatrick, *Writings of Washington*, 21:253–56; Washington to Lafayette, February 25, 1781, Fitzpatrick, *Writings of Washington*, 21:290.

72. George Washington, "Instructions to Marquis de Lafayette," February 20, 1781, Fitzpatrick, *Writings of Washington*, 21:253–56.

73. Washington to Chevalier Destouches, February 22, 1781, Fitzpatrick, *Writings of Washington*, 21:278.

74. Washington to Arthur St. Clair, February 26, 1781, Fitzpatrick, *Writings of Washington*, 21:294.

75. Leibiger, "George Washington and Lafayette: Father and Son of the Revolution," 210–31. For recent biographies of Lafayette, see Leepson, *Lafayette*, and Gaines, *Liberty and Glory*.

76. Washington to Lafayette, 1 March 1781, Founders Online; Tower, *La Fayette*, 2:234.

77. Lafayette to Washington, March 2, 1781, Founders Online.

78. Ibid.; Jefferson to Samuel Huntington, February 17, 1781, Boyd, *Papers of Jefferson*, 4:638–40.

79. Tower, *La Fayette*, 2:226–27.

80. Lafayette to Washington, March 7, 1781, Founders Online.

81. Lafayette to Washington, March 8, 1781, Founders Online.

82. Tower, *La Fayette*, 2:344; Lafayette to Washington, March 9, 1781, Founders Online; Lafayette to Washington, March 15, 1781, Founders Online; Lafayette to Washington, March 23, 1781, Founders Online.

83. Nelson, *Washington's Great Gamble*, 48, 58–71; Tower, *La Fayette*, 2:247; Marquis de Lafayette to Madame de Lafayette, August 24, 1781, Lafayette, *Memoirs*.

84. Tower, *La Fayette*, 2:247, 249, 252–55; Lafayette to Washington, March 26, 1781, Founders Online; Lafayette to Washington, April 5, 1781, Founders Online; Lafayette to Washington, April 6, 1781, Founders Online; Lafayette to Greene, April 4, 1781, Conrad, *Papers of Greene*, 8:51.

85. Greene to Lafayette, April 3, 1781, Conrad, *Papers of Greene*, 8:33–35.

86. Lafayette to Washington, April 8, 1781, Founders Online; Lafayette to Washington, April 10, 1781, Founders Online.

87. Lafayette to Greene, April 4, 1781, Conrad, *Papers of Greene*, 8:107–8.

88. Lafayette to Washington, April 12, 1781, Founders Online; Lafayette to Washington, April 14, 1781, Founders Online; Lafayette to Washington, April 15, 1781, Founders Online; Washington to the Board of War, April 20, 1781, Fitzpatrick, *Writings of Washington*, 21:480; Tower, *La Fayette*, 2:259.

89. Lafayette to Washington, April 18, 1781, Founders Online; Lafayette to Washington, May 5, 1781, Founders Online; Lafayette, *Memoirs*; Lafayette to Greene, April 4, 1781, Conrad, *Papers of Greene*, 8:107–8; Tower, *La Fayette*, 2:258.

90. Lafayette to Washington, April 18, 1781, Founders Online; Lafayette to Washington, April 23, 1781, Founders Online.

91. Lafayette to Jefferson, April 21, 1781, Boyd, *Papers of Jefferson*, 5:522–24.

92. Lafayette to Jefferson, April 25, 1781, Boyd, *Papers of Jefferson*, 5:553–54.

93. Lafayette to Jefferson, April 27, 1781, Boyd, *Papers of Jefferson*, 5:564; Lafayette to Greene, April 28, 1781, Conrad, *Papers of Greene*, 8:171.

94. Greene to Lafayette, May 1, 1781, Conrad, *Papers of Greene*, 8:182–83.

95. Lafayette to Alexander Hamilton, May 23, 1781, Syrett, *Papers of Hamilton*, 2:643–45; Lafayette to Greene, April 28, 1781, Conrad, *Papers of Greene*, 8:171; Lafayette to Greene, May 3, 1781, Conrad, *Papers of Greene*, 8:196.

96. Tower, *La Fayette*, 2:307–11; Arnold to Clinton, May 12, 1781, "Arnold's Expedition to Richmond," 187–90.

97. Lafayette to Greene, May 18, 1781, Conrad, *Papers of Greene*, 8:280–82; Lafayette to Greene, May 24, 1781, Conrad, *Papers of Greene*, 8:308–9.

98. Lafayette to Greene, May 24, 1781, Conrad, *Papers of Greene*, 8:308–9.

99. Richard Henry Lee to George Washington, June 12, 1781, Founders Online; Richard Henry Lee to Virginia Delegates, June 12, 1781, Hutchinson and Rachal, *Papers of James Madison*, 3:156–61.

100. Joseph Jones to George Washington, June 20, 1781, Smith, *Letters of Delegates to Congress*, 17:336–38.

101. Tower, *La Fayette*, 2:314; Lafayette to Washington, May 24, 1781, Founders Online.

102. Lafayette to Washington, May 24, 1781, Founders Online.

103. Ibid.

104. Ibid.

105. Lafayette to Jefferson, May 26, 1781, Boyd, *Papers of Jefferson*, 6:18–19.

106. Joseph Jones to George Washington, June 20, 1781, Smith, *Letters of Delegates to Congress*, 17:336–38.

CHAPTER 4

107. Lafayette to Jefferson, May 26, 1781, Boyd, *Papers of Jefferson*, 6:18–19; Tarleton, *Campaigns*, 292; Tower, *La Fayette*, 2:322.

108. Tarleton, *Campaigns*, 293; *Virginia Gazette*, November 14, 1751; Martin, *Pleasure Gardens of Virginia*, 103.

109. Lafayette to Jefferson, May 26, 1781, Boyd, *Papers of Jefferson*, 6:18–19.

110. Cornwallis to Leslie, May 24, 1781, Saberton, *Cornwallis Papers*, 5:160.

111. Cornwallis to Clinton, May 26, 1781, Saberton, *Cornwallis Papers*, 5:89.

112. Tarleton, *Campaigns*, 293–94; Du Chesnoy, "Campagne en Virginie" (map), Library of Congress Geography and Map Division, Washington, D.C.

113. Tower, *La Fayette*, 2:323–24.

114. Jefferson to Washington, May 28, 1781, Founders Online.

115. Henry Young to William Davies, June 9, 1781, Boyd, *Papers of Jefferson*, 6:84–86.

116. Jefferson, *Notes on the State of Virginia*, 185. It should be noted that the records of the Virginia Assembly for this session do not show that such a motion was presented or debated.

117. Richard Henry Lee to the Virginia Delegates in Congress, June 12, 1781, Boyd, *Papers of Jefferson*, 6:90–93.

118. From Jefferson to the County Lieutenants of Washington and Certain Other Counties, May 28, 1781, Boyd, *Papers of Jefferson*, 6:24–25.

119. Lafayette, *Memoirs*, 1:536.

120. Lafayette to Jefferson, May 28, 1781, Boyd, *Papers of Jefferson*, 6:25–27.

121. "Fredericksburg in Revolutionary Days, Part I."

122. James Hunter to Jefferson, May 30, 1781, Boyd, *Papers of Jefferson*, 6:41.

123. Lafayette to Jefferson, May 28, 1781, Boyd, *Papers of Jefferson*, 6:25–27.

124. Ibid.; Lafayette to Chevalier de la Luzerne, June 16, 1781, Idzerda, *Lafayette*, 4:186.

125. From Jefferson to Lafayette, May 29, 1781, Boyd, *Papers of Jefferson*, 6:35–38.

126. Lafayette to Wayne, May 29, 1781, Idzerda, *Lafayette*, 4:141–42.

127. Lafayette to Jefferson, May 31, 1781, Boyd, *Papers of Jefferson*, 6:52–53; William Langborn to Richard Claiborne, May 31, 1781, Saberton, *Cornwallis Papers*, 5:260–61; David Ross to George Nicolson, June 2, 1781, Saberton, *Cornwallis Papers*, 5:262.

128. See reference files in Central Rappahannock Regional Library, Fredericksburg, under topic heading "Mattaponi Church"; Du Chesnoy, "Campagne en Virginie" (map); Quenzel, *History and Background*, 8–9; Mansfield, *History of Early Spotsylvania*, 58–59, 72, 133.

129. Johnston, *Yorktown Campaign*, 40; Du Chesnoy, "Campagne en Virginie" (map); Corbin's Bridge marker history, http://www.markerhistory.com/lafayette-at-corbins-bridge-jj-7.

130. Lafayette to Wayne, June 2, 1781, Idzerda, *Lafayette*, 4:160.

131. George Weedon to Lafayette, June 1, 1781, Idzerda, *Lafayette*, 4:158; Idzerda, *Lafayette*, 4:495–96; George Weedon to Lafayette, June 4, 1781, in "Fredericksburg in Revolutionary Days, Part II," 167–68.

132. Johnston, *Yorktown Campaign*, 40; Rainey, *Germanna Road*, 23; Tower, *La Fayette*, 2:325.

133. Tarleton, *Campaigns*, 294–99; Lafayette to Greene, June 3, 1781, Idzerda, *Lafayette*, 4:164.

134. Commager and Morris, *Spirit of 'Seventy-Six*, 1,207; Peterson, *Jefferson*, 234; Ferling, *Almost a Miracle*, 512; Gottschalk, *Lafayette*, 431; Tower, *La Fayette*, 2:320.

135. Loth, *Virginia Landmarks*, 219; Hobbs, "History of the Broaddus Flats Site"; Lounsbury, *Courthouses of Early Virginia*, 212; Rice and Brown, *American Campaigns*, 2:102, 175; Simcoe, *Military Journal*, 211.

136. Simcoe, *Military Journal*, 211.

137. Rice and Brown, *Rochambeau's Army*, 2:101–2, 175.

138. Ibid., 2:101; Johnston, *Yorktown Campaign*, 39; "Hanover County Court House Historic District," Nomination Form; Cornwallis to Clinton, June 30, 1781, Saberton, *Cornwallis Papers*, 5:104–7; David Ross to George Nicolson, June 2, 1781, Saberton, *Cornwallis Papers*, 5:262.

139. George Weedon to Lafayette, June 4, 1781, in "Fredericksburg in Revolutionary Days, Part II," 168; Joseph Jones to George Washington, June 20, 1781, Smith, *Letters of Delegates to Congress*, 17:336–38.

140. James Madison to Phili Mazzei, July 7, 1781, Hutchinson and Rachal, *Papers of James Madison*, 3:176–83.

141. King, *Henry Clay*, 5.

142. Simcoe, *Military Journal*, 211.

143. Faden, "Marches of Cornwallis," 1787 map; Cornwallis to Clinton, June 30, 1781, Saberton, *Cornwallis Papers*, 5:104–7. For the unsigned map in the British Library, see reproduced image details in Idzerda, *Lafayette*, 4:163, 232. Although some contemporary sources indicate the British marched from Hanover Court House and crossed the Pamunkey River over Littlepage's Bridge about two miles to the north, it appears that Cornwallis moved instead along the south bank of the North Anna River to a crossing of that river a dozen miles or so to the northwest. At the end of June, Cornwallis reported that he had "moved to Hanover Court House and crossed the South Anna," later reporting that he sent his "light troops over the North Anna" River. If he had crossed the Pamunkey at Littlepage's Bridge, he would not have marched on a route that crossed the South Anna, nor would he have had to have advanced his light troops over the North Anna, as he would already have been on the far side of that stream. This is confirmed by Faden's map in the British Library in London, which depicts Cornwallis's route through Virginia in 1781 and shows that his army did not cross at Littlepage's Bridge but proceeded to the North Anna River from the south.

Chapter 5

144. Lafayette to Greene, June 3, 1781, Idzerda, *Lafayette*, 4:162; Simcoe, *Military Journal*, 211.

145. Maass, "To Disturb the Assembly," 148–57; Tower, *Lafayette*, 2:328–29; Mack, *Life of Gilbert Motier de Lafayette*, 172. Chesterfield Tavern is today's Ruther Glen.

146. Cornwallis to Clinton, June 30, 1781, Saberton, *Cornwallis Papers*, 5:104.

147. Ibid.

148. Jefferson to Virginia Delegates, 14 May 1781, Hutchinson and Rachal, *Papers of James Madison*, 3:120–21; Commonwealth of Virginia, *Journal of the House*, 3.

149. Jefferson to Lafayette, May 14, 1781, Boyd, *Papers of Jefferson*, 5:644–47; Jefferson to James Monroe, May 15, 1781, Boyd, *Papers of Jefferson*, 5:655.

150. Maass, "To Disturb the Assembly," 153; Kranish, *Flight from Monticello*, 269.

151. Commonwealth of Virginia, *Journal of the House*, 3–7; Russell, *Fauquier County*, 415.

152. Jefferson to Washington, May 28, 1781, Founders Online; Malone, *Jefferson*, 354–55; Commonwealth of Virginia, *Journal of the House*, 7–10. Penn's Tavern was located at what is now Clifford, previously known as New Glasgow, on State Route 151 several miles west of U.S. 29.

153. Commonwealth of Virginia, *Journal of the House*, 4, 10; Maass, "To Disturb the Assembly," 154.

154. Simcoe, *Military Journal*, 212; Tarleton, *Campaigns*, 294–95. Point of Fork was located across the Rivanna River from today's Columbia.

155. Cornwallis to Clinton, June 30, 1781, Saberton, *Cornwallis Papers*, 5:104; Tarleton, *Campaigns*, 295; Maass, "To Disturb the Assembly," 153; Lafayette to Greene, June 3, 1781, Idzerda, *Lafayette*, 4:165. Old Albemarle Courthouse was just west of modern Scottsville.

156. Maass, "To Disturb the Assembly," 153; Stedman, *History of the Origin*, 2:387.

157. Tarleton, *Campaigns*, 295–96; Maass, "To Disturb the Assembly," 153–54.

158. "Notes and Documents Relating to the British Invasions in 1781," Boyd, *Papers of Jefferson*, 4:256–78; Maass, "To Disturb the Assembly," 154; Crews, "Captain Jack Jouett's Ride to the Rescue."

159. Maass, "To Disturb the Assembly," 154; Wilson, "Narrow Escape"; Cooper, *Guide to Historic Charlottesville*, 62–64; Merrill, *Jefferson's Nephews*, 25.

160. Joseph Jones to George Washington, June 20, 1781, Smith, *Letters of Delegates to Congress*, 17:336–38.

161. Tarleton, *Campaigns*, 296.

162. Ambler, "Old Virginia Correspondence."

163. Tarleton, *Campaigns*, 296; Maass, "To Disturb the Assembly," 154; Kranish, *Flight from Monticello*, 277; Lewis of Warner Hall, *History of a Family*, 601; Lancaster, *Homes and Churches*, 399–400; Long, "Drama on the Plantations"; James Madison to Phili Mazzei, July 7, 1781, Smith, *Letters of Delegates to Congress*, 17:381–86.

164. Lancaster, *Homes and Churches*, 396; Kukla, *Mister Jefferson's Women*, 12, 41–44, 49, 53; Henderson, "Dr. Thomas Walker"; Dabney, "Jouett Outrides Tarleton."

165. Tarleton, *Campaigns*, 296.

166. Kranish, *Flight from Monticello*, 276; Long, "Drama on the Plantations"; Maass, "To Disturb the Assembly," 154.

167. Tarleton, *Campaigns*, 297; Merrill, *Jefferson's Nephews*, 26.

168. Wyllie, *Daniel Boone's Adventures*; Maass, "To Disturb the Assembly," 154; Hammon, *My Father, Daniel Boone*, 72–73; Lofaro, *Daniel Boone*, 118.

169. Tarleton, *Campaigns*, 297–98.

170. Lee to Delegates, June 12, 1781, Hutchinson and Rachal, *Papers of James Madison*, 3:156–61.

171. Tarleton, *Campaigns*, 297.

172. Maass, "To Disturb the Assembly," 155–56; Merrill, *Jefferson's Nephews*, 24.

173. Richard Henry Lee to Virginia Delegates, June 12, 1781, Hutchinson and Rachal, *Papers of James Madison*, 3:156–61.

174. Hayes, *Road to Monticello*, 232; Burstein and Isenberg, *Jefferson and Madison*, 82.

175. Kranish, *Flight from Monticello*, 283; Randall, *Jefferson*, 1:337.

176. Cogliano, *Emperor of Liberty*, 25–26; Kranish, *Flight from Monticello*, 283; Hudson, Statement, July 26, 1805.

177. Kranish, *Flight from Monticello*, 280; Peterson, *Jefferson*, 235–36, 279; Randall, *Jefferson*, 1:337.

178. "Diary of Arnold's Invasion and Notes on Subsequent Events in 1781: Versions of 1796?, 1805, and 1816," Boyd, *Papers of Jefferson*, 4:258–68.

179. Burstein and Isenberg, *Jefferson and Madison*, 82.

180. Ferling, *Jefferson and Hamilton*, 115–17; Randall, *Jefferson*, 1:338–39.

181. Washington, *Writings of Thomas Jefferson*, 2:425–26.

182. Cogliano, *Emperor of Liberty*, 26; Gordon-Reed, *Hemingses of Monticello*, 139.

183. Peterson, *Jefferson*, 236.

184. Kranish, *Flight from Monticello*, 285–86; Hayes, *Road to Monticello*, 232–33.

185. Simcoe, *Military Journal*, 212.

186. Ibid.

187. Ibid., 212–16.

188. Von Steuben to Lafayette, June 5, 1781, Idzerda, *Lafayette*, 4:170.

189. Simcoe, *Military Journal*, 217.

190. Ibid., 218; Mitchell Pension Application, January 28, 1833.

191. Simcoe, *Military Journal*, 219.

192. Ibid., 221–22; Maass, "Greatest Terror Imaginable"; Lee, *Memoirs of the War*, 423.

193. David Ross to William Davies, June 28, 1781, Palmer, *Calendar of State Papers*, 2:188; Maass, "Greatest Terror Imaginable," 42–47.

194. Simcoe, *Military Journal*, 222–23; Cornwallis to Clinton, June 30, 1781, Saberton, *Cornwallis Papers*, 5:104.

195. Tarleton, *Campaigns*, 306.

196. Ibid., 295.

197. Cornwallis to Clinton, June 30, 1781, Saberton, *Cornwallis Papers*, 5:104; Washington to Arthur St. Clair, June 23, 1781, Fitzpatrick, *Writings of Washington*, 22:253.

198. Maass, "Greatest Terror Imaginable," 48–49.

199. MacMaster, "News of the Yorktown Campaign."

200. Maass, "Greatest Terror Imaginable," 50–53; Virginia Conservation Commission, *Virginia*, 620.

201. Bates Petition, October 11, 1782.

202. Richard Henry Lee to William Lee, July 15, 1781, in Ballagh, *Letters of Richard Henry Lee*, 2:242–44; Urwin, "Cornwallis and the Slaves of Virginia," 172–92; Nash, *Unknown American Revolution*, 336.

203. Pybus, "Jefferson's Faulty Math."

204. Urwin, "Cornwallis and the Slaves of Virginia," 172–92; Urwin, "When Freedom Wore a Red Coat," *Army History*, Summer 2008: 6–23.

205. Pybus, "Jefferson's Faulty Math," 243–64; Nash, *Unknown American Revolution*, 338; Cornwallis to Thomas Nelson Jr., August 6, 1781, Saberton, *Cornwallis Papers*, 6:86–87; Capon, *Atlas of Early American History*, 97.

206. Lafayette to Washington, July 20, 1781, Idzerda, *Lafayette*, 4:255–57; Ewald, *Diary of the American War*, 305.

207. McDonnell, *Politics of War*, 476; Taylor, *Internal Enemy*, 27–28; Hiden, "Losses of York County Citizens."

208. Cornwallis to Tarleton, June 5, 1781, Saberton, *Cornwallis Papers*, 5:225.

209. Malone, *Jefferson*, 441–42; map, "March of the Army under Lieut. General Earl Cornwallis in Virginia…," Manuscripts Department, British Library, London, reproduced in Idzerda, *Lafayette*, 4:163; Maass, "Greatest Terror Imaginable," 60.

210. Weeks, "Thomas Jefferson's Elk-Hill." The details of the house and a map of the property given in Jefferson's hand are found in "Advertisement for sale of Elk-hill lands," a 1790 manuscript in the Coolidge Collection of the Massachusetts Historical Society and reproduced in Maass, "Greatest Terror Imaginable," 58–59.

211. Thomas Jefferson to William Gordon, July 16, 1788, Boyd, *Papers of Jefferson*, 13:363–64.

212. Maass, "Greatest Terror Imaginable," 64.

213. Parton, *Life of Thomas Jefferson*, 254; Kranish, *Flight from Monticello*, 292–93.

214. Simcoe, *Military Journal*, 224. The storehouses at Seven Islands were in Fluvanna County at the end of Route 640, about six miles south of Kidds Store.

215. Tarleton, *Campaigns*, 298–99, 344–45; Ford, *Phase I Archaeological and Geophysical Survey*, 10–32. The site of the old courthouse is on Route 726, between that county road and the river, one mile from Scottsville.

216. Tarleton, *Campaigns*, 345–46.

Chapter 6

217. Blackwell Pension Application, December 6, 1833; Lafayette to Greene, June 3, 1781, Idzerda, *Lafayette*, 4:162–65.

218. Cockburn, *Journey Through Hallowed Ground*, 59. Germanna Ford is at the Route 3 bridge on the Rapidan River, nine and a half miles west of the Chancellorsville Battlefield Visitors' Center.

219. For text of Virginia Marker OC22, see http://www.markerhistory.com/the-campaign-of-1781-lafayettes-maneuvers-marker-oc-22.

220. Fiske, *American Revolution*, 2:272.

221. William Constable to Thomas Drew, June 4, 1781, Saberton, *Cornwallis Papers*, 5:264.

222. Idzerda, *Lafayette*, 4:496.

223. Papageorgiou, *Colonial Churches*, 7–9; Slaughter, *History of St. Mark's Parish*, 15.

224. Idzerda, *Lafayette*, 4:496.

225. Lafayette to Wayne, June 6, 1781, Idzerda, *Lafayette*, 4:171–72; Wayne to Lafayette, June 7, 1781, ibid.

226. "Campaign of 1781," Markerhistory.com, http://www.markerhistory.com/campaign-of-1781-marker-jj-24.

227. Lafayette to Washington, June 10, 1781, Founders Online.

228. Anthony Wayne to George Washington, January 2, 1781, Founders Online.

229. Wright, *Continental Army*, 151–63; Wayne to Washington, January 21, 1781, Founders Online; Trussell, *Pennsylvania Line*, 18, 209.

230. Wayne to Washington, March 19, 1781, Founders Online; Thomas Rodney's Diary, April 12, 1781, Smith, *Letters to Delegates to the Congress*, 17:145–46.

231. Washington to Wayne, April 8, 1781, Fitzpatrick, *Writings of Washington*, 21:432–33; Washington to Jefferson, April 18, 1781, ibid., 21:473.

232. Tucker, *Mad Anthony Wayne and the New Nation*, 192–93; Shepard, *Marching to Victory*, 7; Denny, *Military Journal*, 33–34; Egle, "Journal of Lieut. William McDowell," 15:297.

233. Wayne to Lafayette, May 31, 1781, Idzerda, *Lafayette*, 4:156–57.

234. Wayne to Lafayette, June 1, 1781, Idzerda, *Lafayette*, 4:156–57, 4:157; Feltman, *Journal*, 3; Lee Shepard, *Marching to Victory*, 8.

235. Feltman, *Journal*, 4; Shepard, *Marching to Victory*, 8.

236. Wayne to Lafayette, June 4, 1781, Idzerda, *Lafayette*, 4:169; Feltman, *Journal*, 4; Toler, "Remembering Red House"; Shepard, *Marching to Victory*, 8; Denny, *Military Journal*, 35. "The Red House" was located at today's Haymarket.

237. Shepard, *Marching to Victory*, 9; Auburn Civil War Battlefield District application.

238. Episcopal Diocese of Virginia website, http://www.thediocese.net/news/newsView.asp?NewsId=40968223; Elk Run Site Preservation Committee website, http://www.elkrunchurch.org/about; Wayne to Lafayette, June 6, 1781, Idzerda, *Lafayette*, 4:171; Shepard, *Marching to*

Victory, 9. The author wishes to thank Ed Dandar of the Elk Run Church Preservation Committee for providing information about this colonial church.

239. Wayne to Lafayette, June 7, 1781, Idzerda, *Lafayette*, 4:172; Feltman, *Journal*, 4. York was today's Stevensburg.

240. Idzerda, *Lafayette*, xliv; Felton, *Journal*, 4; Nelson, *Anthony Wayne*, 134; Shepard, *Marching to Victory*, 9; Tower, *La Fayette*, 2:328; Gottschalk, *Lafayette*, 243; Waddell, "Diary of Captain John Davis"; Lafayette to Chevalier de la Luzerne, June 16, 1781, Idzerda, *Lafayette*, 4:186; Denny, *Military Journal*, 35; Egle, "Journal of Lieut. William McDowell," 298.

241. Idzerda, *Lafayette*, xliv; Felton, *Journal*, 4; Nelson, *Anthony Wayne*, 134; Shepard, *Marching to Victory*, 9; Egle, "Journal of Lieut. William McDowell," 298; Tower, *La Fayette*, 2:328; Gottschalk, *Lafayette*, 243; Waddell, "Diary of Captain John Davis"; Lafayette to Daniel Morgan, June 12, 1781, Idzerda, *Lafayette*, 4:176.

242. Idzerda, *Lafayette*, 4:496. The road north of the bridge for several miles is now called "Marquis Road."

243. Johnston, *Yorktown Campaign*, 47.

244. Ibid.

245. Lafayette to Daniel Morgan, June 12, 1781, Idzerda, *Lafayette*, 4:176; Johnston, *Yorktown Campaign*, 47; Feltman, *Journal*, 4; Waddell, "Diary of Captain John Davis."

246. Lafayette to Nathanael Greene, June 18, 1781, Idzerda, *Lafayette*, 4:192–93; Lafayette to Greene, June 20, 1781, ibid., 4:197–200.

247. Maass, "Greatest Terror Imaginable," 64–66.

248. Cornwallis to Clinton, June 30, 1781, Saberton, *Cornwallis Papers*, 104; Lafayette to Greene, June 18, 1781, Idzerda, *Lafayette*, 4:193.

249. Idzerda, *Lafayette*, 4:163 (map), and Lafayette to Greene, June 18, 1781, ibid., 4:191–93; Simcoe, *Military Journal*, 223–24; Maass, "Greatest Terror Imaginable," 67–68; "British Orderly Book" (the author wishes to thank Gregory J. Urwin for bringing this orderly book to his attention).

250. Maass, "Greatest Terror Imaginable," 67–68; "Mount Bernard Complex," National Register of Historic Places Registration Form; Griffin Petition, Library of Virginia.

251. Simcoe, *Military Journal*, 224; Idzerda, *Lafayette*, 4:163 (map); Tarleton, *Campaigns*, 300.

252. Lafayette to Baron von Steuben, June 13, 1781, Idzerda, *Lafayette*, 4:179–80.

253. Lafayette to la Luzerne, June 16, 1781, Idzerda, *Lafayette Papers*, 4:186.

254. Lafayette to Daniel Morgan, June 12, 1781, Idzerda, *Lafayette*, 4:176; Lafayette to Greene, June 18, 1781, ibid., 4:192–93; Lafayette to Washington, June 18, 1781, ibid., 4:195; Lafayette to la Luzerne, June 16, 1781, ibid., 4:186.

255. Ibid., 4:187–88.

256. William Fleming to Thomas Jefferson, June 14, 1781, Thomas Jefferson Papers, LOC.

257. Idzerda, *Lafayette*, 4:496; Lafayette to George Weedon, June 16, 1781, ibid., 4:189; Nelson, Pension Application.

258. "Fredericksburg in Revolutionary Days, Part II," 164–75.

259. Lafayette to Baron von Steuben, June 13, 1781, Idzerda, *Lafayette*, 4:179–80; Lafayette to Washington, June 18, 1781, ibid., 4:195.

260. Lafayette to la Luzerne, June 16, 1781, Idzerda, *Lafayette*, 4:186. Cole's Ferry in Halifax County was about ten miles southeast of modern Brookneal.

261. Lafayette to Washington, June 18, 1781, Idzerda, *Lafayette*, 4:194.

262. Ibid., 4:195.

263. Lafayette to la Luzerne, June 16, 1781, Idzerda, *Lafayette*, 4:188.

264. Joseph Jones to Washington, June 20, 1781, Smith, *Letters of Delegates to Congress*, 17:336–38.

265. Lafayette to Greene, July 4, 1781, Idzerda, *Lafayette*, 4:231; Lafayette to von Steuben, October 26, 1781, ibid., 4:432–33; Archibald Cary to Jefferson, June 19, 1781, Boyd, *Papers of Jefferson*, 6:96–98.

266. Von Steuben to Lafayette, June 13, 1781, Idzerda, *Lafayette*, 4:182.

267. Lafayette to Daniel Morgan, June 12, 1781, Idzerda, *Lafayette*, 4:176.

268. Lafayette to la Luzerne, June 16, 1781, Idzerda, *Lafayette*, 4:186; Feltman, *Journal*, 4; Waddell, "Diary of Captain John Davis"; Egle, "Journal of Lieut. William McDowell," 298.

269. Idzerda, *Lafayette*, 4:176; Chesnoy map; Feltman, *Journal*, 4; Shepard, *Marching to Victory*, 9.

270. Lafayette to la Luzerne, June 16, 1781, Idzerda, *Lafayette*, 4:186.

271. Lafayette to George Weedon, June 16, 1781, Idzerda, *Lafayette*, 4:189.

272. Ibid.; "Fredericksburg in Revolutionary Days, Part II," 164–75.

273. Weedon to Lafayette, June 17, 1781, Idzerda, *Lafayette*, 4:190–91.

274. Maass, "Greatest Terror Imaginable," 79–81; Feltman, *Journal*, 4; Egle, "Journal of Lieut. William McDowell," 298.

275. Lafayette to Washington, June 18, 1781, Idzerda, *Lafayette*, 4:195; Beakes, "Service of Colonel William Campbell"; Johnston, *Yorktown Campaign*, 52–53.

276. Lafayette to Greene, June 20, 1781, Idzerda, *Lafayette*, 4:198; Tarleton, *Campaigns*, 300; Feltman, *Journal*, 4; Waddell, "Diary of Captain John Davis"; Shepard, *Marching to Victory*, 10.

277. Tarleton, *Campaigns*, 300; Idzerda, *Lafayette*, 4:163 (map); Lafayette to Wayne, June 21, 1781, Idzerda, *Lafayette*, 4:205; Feltman, *Journal*, 5.

278. Lafayette to Greene, June 21, 1781, Idzerda, *Lafayette*, 4:203–4.

279. Greene to Lafayette, June 23, 1781, Idzerda, *Lafayette*, 4:209; Feltman, *Journal*, 5.

280. Fry and Jefferson, "Map of the Inhabited Part of Virginia"; Hiden, "Losses of York County," 132–35.

281. Lafayette to von Steuben, June 22, 1781, Idzerda, *Lafayette*, 4:206.

282. Lafayette to Wayne, June 22, 1781, ibid., 4:206–7.

283. Wayne to Lafayette, June 22, 1781, ibid., 4:207–8.

284. Feltman, *Journal*, 5.

285. Ibid.; Waddell, "Diary of Captain John Davis"; Shepard, *March to Victory*, 10; Denny, *Journal*, 35–36.

286. Waddell, "Diary of Captain John Davis"; Feltman, *Journal*, 5.

287. Shepard, *March to Victory*, 10–11.

288. Johnston, "Christian Febiger"; Trussell, *Pennsylvania Line*, 219.

289. Tarleton, *Campaigns*, 300–301; British map, Idzerda, *Lafayette*, 4:233; Cornwallis to Clinton, June 30, 1781, Saberton, *Cornwallis Papers*, 5:104.

CHAPTER 7

290. Johnston, *Yorktown Campaign*, 56; Ward, *War of the Revolution*, 2:875; Feltman, *Journal*, 6; Egle, "Journal of Lieut. William McDowell," 300.

291. Simcoe *Military Journal*, 229; Johnston, *Yorktown Campaign*, 56; Feltman, *Journal*, 6; Egle, "Journal of Lieut. William McDowell," 300.

292. Johnston, *Yorktown Campaign*, 56; Simcoe, *Military Journal*, 229–36; McAllister, *Virginia Militia*, 86, 111. Tyree's Plantation was near today's Lanexa, north of U.S. Route 60.

293. Lafayette to Thomas Nelson, June 28, 1781, Rockefeller Library.

294. Ibid.; Morrissey, *Yorktown 1781*, 25, 39, 43; Lafayette to Greene, Idzerda, *Lafayette*, 4:216.

295. Tower, *La Fayette*, 2:351.

296. Lafayette to Thomas Nelson Jr., July 1, 1781, Idzerda, *Lafayette*, 4:228–31.

297. Tower, *La Fayette*, 2:354–55; Lafayette to Greene, July 4, 1781, Idzerda, *Lafayette*, 4:231.

298. Lafayette to Greene, July 4, 1781, Idzerda, *Lafayette*, 4:234.

299. Tower, *La Fayette*, 2:355–56; Cornwallis to Clinton, Ross, *Correspondence of Cornwallis*, 1:103–6.

300. Tower, *La Fayette*, 2:356.

301. Ibid., 356–57, 361; Anthony Wayne to George Washington, July 8, 1781, Founders Online; quote regarding Green Spring house is of the architect Benjamin Latrobe, given at the National Park Service's "Green Spring Plantation" webpage, http://www.nps.gov/jame/historyculture/green-spring-plantation.htm.

302. Tower, *La Fayette*, 360.

303. Ibid., 361; Shepard, *Marching to Victory*, 13; Ward, *War of the Revolution*, 2:876.

304. Wayne to Washington, July 8, 1781, Founders Online.

305. Ibid.; Shepard, *Marching to Victory*, 13; Egle, "Journal of Lieut. William McDowell," 301.

306. Tower, *La Fayette*, 362–64; Cornwallis to Clinton, July 8, 1781, Ross, *Correspondence of Cornwallis*, 1:106; Ward, *War of the Revolution*, 2:477; Idzerda, *Lafayette*, 4:238n; Cornwallis to Nesbit Balfour, July 16, 1781, Saberton, *Cornwallis Papers*, 5:285.

307. Shepard, *Marching to Victory*, 13; Tower, *La Fayette*, 366.

308. Lafayette to Greene, July 8, 1781, Idzerda, *Lafayette*, 4:238, 239.

309. Wayne to Washington, July 8, 1781, Founders Online.

310. Lafayette, General Orders, July 8, 1781, Idzerda, *Lafayette*, 4:240; Lafayette to Allen Jones, July 10, 1781, ibid., 4:241.

311. Lafeyette, *Memoirs*, 1:420; Lafayette to the Vicomte de Noailles, July 10, 1781, Idzerda, *Lafayette*, 4:241.

312. Cornwallis to Clinton, July 8, 1781, Saberton, *Cornwallis Papers*, 5:117.

313. Clinton to Cornwallis, July 8, 1781, Saberton, *Cornwallis Papers*, 5:141; Clinton to Cornwallis, July 11, 1781, ibid., 5:139, 142–43.

314. Cornwallis to Clinton, July 17, 1781, Saberton, *Cornwallis Papers*, 5:137.

315. Ibid., 5:138; Cornwallis to Tarleton, July 8, 1781, ibid., 5:228.

316. "Peter Francisco, American Soldier."

317. Mapp, *Thomas Jefferson*, 160; Tarleton, *Campaigns*, 369; Hendricks, *Backcountry Towns*, 74–76. New London was just south of the current city limits of Lynchburg, along U.S. Route 460 at Route 811, New London Road.

318. Tarleton, *Campaigns*, 369.

319. Bell, *Cumberland Parish*, 105–8; Craig's Mill was located two miles south of modern Kenbridge, on Route 637.

320. Tarleton, *Campaigns*, 369–70; Morrissey, *Yorktown 1781*, 43; *Virginia Gazette*, March 23 1775, 4; Lafayette to Morgan, July 17, 1781, Idzerda, *Lafayette*, 4:253; Lafayette to Wayne, July 25, 1781, Idzerda, *Lafayette*, 4:278.

321. Lafayette to Nelson, July 13, 1781, Idzerda, *Lafayette*, 4:244–45; Wayne to Washington, July 16, 1781, Founders Online; Lafayette to Washington July 20, 1781, Idzerda, *Lafayette*, 4:255–56.

322. Lafayette to Wayne, July 15, 1781, Idzerda, *Lafayette*, 4:248–49; Lafayette to Morgan, July 16, 1781, ibid., 4:251. Goode's Bridge is where U.S. 360 passes over the Appomattox River in western Chesterfield County.

323. Shepard, *Marching to Victory*, 14–16.

324. Lafayette to Washington, July 20, 1781, Idzerda, *Lafayette*, 4:255–57; Lafayette to Greene, July 23, 1781, ibid., 4:269–70.

325. Lafayette to William Davies, July 27, 1781, Idzerda, *Lafayette*, 4:279.

326. Lafayette to Washington, July 30, 1781, Idzerda, *Lafayette*, 4:86–87; Shepard, *Marching to Victory*, 15; Idzerda, *Lafayette*, 504.

327. Cornwallis to Clinton, July 24, 1781, Saberton, *Cornwallis Papers*, 6:11–13, 27–28; Josiah Parker to Lafayette, August 19, 1781, Idzerda, *Lafayette*, 4:334.

328. Lafayette to Wayne, August 4, 1781, Idzerda, *Lafayette*, 4:294; Feltman, *Journal*, 9; Wayne to Lafayette, August 9, 1781, Idzerda, *Lafayette*, 4:307; Lafayette to Greene, August 12, 1781, Idzerda, *Lafayette*, 4:315–17; Morrissey, *Yorktown 1781*, 36; Lafayette to the Prince e Poix, August 24, 1781, Idzerda, *Lafayette*, 4:346–47; Lafayette to La Luzerne, August 14, 1781, Idzerda, *Lafayette*, 4:321–22. Lafayette's Continentals were encamped during this period along Sweet Hall Road, south of King William Road (Route 30).

329. Lafayette to La Luzerne, August 14, 1781, Idzerda, *Lafayette*, 4:321–22.

CHAPTER 8

330. Tower, *La Fayette*, 2:381–89; Selig, *March to Victory*, 3, 9–10.

331. Tower, *La Fayette*, 2:383–85; Selig, *March to Victory*, 11.

332. Tower, *La Fayette*, 2:390–91, 399–400; Selig, *March to Victory*, 13, 15.

333. Selig, *March to Victory*, 22; Tower, *La Fayette*, 2:395.

334. Tower, *La Fayette*, 2:401–3; Selig, *March to Victory*, 23.

335. Tower, *La Fayette*, 2:404–5, 419–20, 427; Washington to Lafayette, August 21, 1781, Idzerda, *Lafayette*, 4:340.

336. Tower, *La Fayette*, 2:427–30; Lafayette to Nelson, August 30, 1781, Idzerda, *Lafayette*, 4:369–71.

337. Tower, *La Fayette*, 2:423, 429, 435; De Grasse to Lafayette, August 30, 1781, Idzerda, *Lafayette*, 4:375; Feltman *Journal*, 12.

338. Tower, *La Fayette*, 2:430–32.

339. Ibid., 2:432; Lafayette to Samuel Cooper, October 26, 1781, Idzerda, *Lafayette*, 4:429.

340. Lafayette to Samuel Cooper, October 26, 1781, Idzerda, *Lafayette*, 4:429.

341. Resolution of Congress, November 23, 1781, Idzerda, *Lafayette*, 4:440.

342. Thomas Nelson Jr. to George Washington, July 27, 1781, Founders Online.

CODA

343. John Beckley to Thomas Jefferson, June 12, 1781, Boyd, *Papers of Jefferson*, 6:88–90; Thomas Jefferson's Governorship of Virginia, Thomas Jefferson Papers, LOC.

344. Archibald Cary to Thomas Jefferson, June 19, 1781, Boyd, *Papers of Jefferson*, 6:96–98.

345. Greene to William Davies, April 11, 1781, Conrad, *Papers of Greene*, 8:80–81.

346. Marquis de Lafayette to George Washington, September 8, 1781, Founders Online.

347. Thomas Jefferson to George Nicholas, July 28, 1781, Boyd, *Papers of Jefferson*, 6:104–5.

348. See interpretive notes to Beckley's letter to Jefferson on June 12, 1781, at Thomas Jefferson Papers, LOC; Malone, *Jefferson*, 362–63.

349. Thomas Jefferson to Edmund Randolph, September 16, 1781, Boyd, *Papers of Jefferson*, 6:117–18; Jefferson to Lafayette, August 4, 1781, Idzerda, *Lafayette*, 4:297.

350. George Nicholas to Thomas Jefferson, July 31, 1781, Boyd, *Papers of Jefferson*, 6:105–6.

351. Malone, *Jefferson the Virginian*, 365–67; *Journal of the House of Delegates of Virginia*, December 12, 1781.

352. Malone, *Jefferson*, 367–68.

353. Thomas Jefferson to George Washington, May 28, 1781, Founders Online; Kimball, *Jefferson*, 242, 244.

354. Richard Henry Lee to George Washington, June 12, 1781, Founders Online.

355. Richard Henry Lee to Virginia Delegates, June 12, 1781, Hutchinson and Rachal, *Papers of James Madison*, 3:156–61.

356. Ambler "Old Virginia Correspondence," 538–39; Malone, *Jefferson*, 358–60; Kimball, *Jefferson*, 243.

357. Conrad, "Lafayette and Cornwallis"; Lerche, "Jefferson and the Election."

358. Washington, *Writings of Jefferson*, 10:219–20, 224; Kimball, *Jefferson*, 245.

359. Washington, *Writings of Jefferson*, 10:225.

BIBLIOGRAPHY

Ambler, Eliza Jacquelin. "An Old Virginia Correspondence." *Atlantic Monthly* 84 (October 1899): 538–39.

"Arnold's Expedition to Richmond, Virginia, 1781." *William and Mary Quarterly*, 2nd ser., 12, no. 3 (July 1932): 187–90.

"Arnold's Invasion, 1781." *William and Mary Quarterly*, 2nd ser., 6, no. 2 (April 1926): 131–32.

Auburn Civil War Battlefield District application for Virginia Landmarks Register. DHR ID #: 030-15140, April 14, 2009.

Ballagh, James C., ed. *The Letters of Richard Henry Lee*. 2 vols. New York: Macmillan Co., 1911–14.

Bates, Thomas. Petition to Virginia legislature, October 11, 1782. Legislative Petitions, Goochland County, Library of Virginia, Richmond, Virginia.

Beakes, John. "The Service of Colonel William Campbell of Virginia." *Journal of the American Revolution*, June 18, 2014. http://allthingsliberty. com/2014/06/the-service-of-colonel-william-campbell-of-virginia.

Bell, Landon Covington. *Cumberland Parish, Lunenburg County, Virginia, 1746–1816*. Richmond, VA: Genealogical Publishing Co., 1930.

Bell, William G. *Commanding Generals and Chiefs of Staff, 1775–2010*. Washington, D.C.: U.S. Army Center of Military History, 2010.

Blackwell, John. Revolutionary War Pension Application, S30873, December 6, 1833. http://www.revwarapps.org.

Boyd, Julian P., ed. *The Papers of Thomas Jefferson*. Princeton, NJ: Princeton University Press, 1950–.

"British Orderly Book, H.B.M. 43d Regiment of Foot, General Orders, May 23 to August 25, 1781." Manuscript 42, 449, MSS 28-29, British Museum, London.

Burstein, Andrew, and Nancy Isenberg. *Jefferson and Madison*. New York: Random House, 2013.

Capon, Lester J., ed. *Atlas of Early American History: The Revolutionary Era, 1760–1790*. Princeton, NJ: Princeton University Press, 1976.

Carrington, Henry B. *Battles of the American Revolution, 1775–1781*. New York: A.S. Barnes & Co., 1877.

Chase, Philander D., ed. *The Papers of George Washington*. Revolutionary War Series. 22 vols. to date. Charlottesville: University Press of Virginia, 1985–.

Clark, Walter, ed. *The State Records of North Carolina*. Vols. 16–26. Raleigh, NC: P.M. Hale, 1886–1907.

Clary, David A., and Joseph W.A. Whitehorne. *The Inspectors General of the United States Army, 1777–1903*. Washington, D.C.: U.S. Army Center of Military History, 1987.

Coakley, Robert W., and Stetson Conn. *The War of the American Revolution*. Washington, D.C.: U.S. Army Center of Military History, 1975.

Cockburn, Andrew. *Journey Through Hallowed Ground: Birthplace of the American Ideal*. Washington, D.C.: National Geographic Books, 2008.

Cogliano, Francis D. *Emperor of Liberty: Thomas Jefferson's Foreign Policy*. New Haven, CT: Yale University Press, 2014.

Commager, Henry Steele, and Richard B. Morris. *The Spirit of 'Seventy-Six*. New York: Harper & Row, 1967.

Commonwealth of Virginia. *Journal of the House of Delegates of the State of Virginia, May 1781*. Richmond, VA: Thomas W. White, 1828.

Conrad, Bryan. "Lafayette and Cornwallis in Virginia, 1781." *William and Mary Quarterly*, 2nd ser., 14, no. 2 (April 1934): 99–104.

Conrad, Dennis, et al., eds. *The Papers of General Nathanael Greene*. 13 vols. Chapel Hill: University of North Carolina Press, 1976–2005.

Cooper, Jean L. *A Guide to Historic Charlottesville and Albemarle County, Virginia*. Charleston, SC: The History Press, 2007.

Crews, Ed. "Captain Jack Jouett's Ride to the Rescue." *Colonial Williamsburg Journal*, Summer 2006. http://www.history.org/Foundation/journal/Summer06/ride.cfm#top.

Dabney, Virginius. "Jouett Outrides Tarleton and Saves Jefferson From Capture." *Scribners* (June 1928): 690–97.

Davies, K.G., ed. *Transcripts 1781*. Vol. 20, *Documents of the American Revolution 1770–1783*. Colonial Office Series. Dublin: Irish University Press, 1972.

Davis, Robert P. *Where a Man Can Go: Major General William Phillips, British Royal Artillery, 1731–1781.* Westport, CT: Greenwood Press, 1999.

Denny, Ebenezer. *Military Journal of Major Ebenezer Denny.* Philadelphia: J.B. Lippincott, 1860.

Du Chesnoy, Capitaine Michel. "Campagne en Virginie du Major Général M'is de LaFayette: Ou Se Trouvent les Camps et Marches, Ainsy Que Ceux du Lieutenant Général Lord Cornwallis en 1781" (map). Library of Congress, call number G3881.S3 1781 .C3.

Egle, W.H., ed. "Journal of Lieut. William McDowell…" *Pennsylvania Archives,* 2nd ser. Harrisburg, PA: E.K. Meyers, State Printer, 1890.

Ewald, Johann von. *Diary of the American War: A Hessian Journal.* Translated and edited by Joseph P. Tustin. New Haven, CT: Yale University Press, 1979.

"Extracts from Journals of Virginia House of Delegates, November 30, 1781." Thomas Jefferson's Governorship of Virginia, Thomas Jefferson Papers, ser. 1, Library of Congress, http://hdl.loc.gov/loc.mss/mtj.mtjbib000677.

Faden, William. "The Marches of Lord Cornwallis in the Southern Provinces, Now States of North America," 1787 map. Library of Congress Geography and Map Division, call number G3861.S3 1787 .F3.

Feltman, William. *The Journal of Lieut. William Feltman of the First Pennsylvania Regiment, 1781–82.* Philadelphia: Henry Carey Baird, 1853.

Ferling, John. *Almost a Miracle: The American Victory in the War of Independence.* New York: Oxford University Press, 2007.

———. *Jefferson and Hamilton: The Rivalry That Forged a Nation.* New York: Bloomsbury Publishing, 2013.

Fiske, John. *The American Revolution.* 2 vols. Boston: Houghton, Mifflin, and Co., 1891.

Fitzpatrick, John C., ed. *Writings of George Washington, from the Original Manuscript Sources, 1745–1799.* 39 vols. Washington, D.C.: U.S. Government Printing Office, 1931–44.

Ford, Benjamin P. *Phase I Archaeological and Geophysical Survey at the Albemarle County Court at Valmont, 002-0443.* Charlottesville, VA: Rivanna Archaeological Services, 2012.

Founders Online, National Archives and Records Administration. http://founders.archives.gov.

"Fredericksburg in Revolutionary Days, Part I." *William and Mary Quarterly* 27, no. 2 (October 1918): 73–95.

"Fredericksburg in Revolutionary Days, Part II." *William and Mary Quarterly* 27, no. 3 (January 1919): 164–75.

Fry, Joshua, and Peter Jefferson. "A Map of the Inhabited Part of Virginia Containing the Whole Province of Maryland, with Part of Pennsylvania, New Jersey and North Carolina," 1753. http://www. EncyclopediaVirginia.org/Fry-Jefferson_Map_of_Virginia.

Gaines, James R. *Liberty and Glory: Washington, Lafayette, and Their Revolutions.* New York: W.W. Norton & Company, 2007.

Gordon-Reed, Annette. *The Hemingses of Monticello: An American Family.* New York: W.W. Norton & Company, 2009.

Gottschalk, Louis. *Lafayette and the Close of the American Revolution.* Chicago: University of Chicago Press, 1942.

Griffin, John Tayloe. Legislative Petition, September 27, 1783. Library of Virginia, Richmond, Virginia.

Gruber, Ira D., ed. *John Peebles' American War: The Diary of a Scottish Grenadier, 1776–1782.* Mechanicsburg, PA: Stackpole Books, 1998.

Hammon, Neal O., ed. *My Father, Daniel Boone: The Draper Interviews with Nathan Boone.* Lexington: University Press of Kentucky Press, 2013.

"Hanover County Court House Historic District." National Register of Historic Places Inventory—Nomination Form. http://www.dhr.virginia. gov/registers/Counties/Hanover/042-0086_Hanover_Court_House_ Historic_District_1971_Final_Nomination.pdf.

Hayes, Kevin J. *The Road to Monticello: The Life and Mind of Thomas Jefferson.* New York: Oxford University Press, 2008.

Henderson, Archibald. "Dr. Thomas Walker and the Loyal Company of Virginia." *American Antiquarian Society* (April 1931): 77–178.

Hendricks, Christopher E. *The Backcountry Towns of Colonial Virginia.* Knoxville: University of Tennessee Press, 2006.

Hiden, P.W. "Losses of York County Citizens in British Invasion, 1781." *William and Mary Quarterly*, 2nd ser., 7, no. 2 (April 1927): 132–35.

Hobbs, Tom. "The History of the Broaddus Flats Site." Virginia Digs. http://www.virginiadigs.net/broaddus_flats/essays/history.html.

Hudson, Christopher. Statement, July 26, 1805. Accession 33598. Personal Papers Collection, Virginia State Library and Archives, Richmond, Virginia.

Hutchinson, William T., and William M.E. Rachal, eds. *The Papers of James Madison.* 33 vols. Chicago: University of Chicago Press, 1962.

Idzerda, Stanley J., ed. *Lafayette in the Age of the American Revolution: Selected Letters and Papers, 1776–1790.* 4 vols. Ithaca, NY: Cornell University Press, 1983.

Jefferson, Thomas. *Notes on the State of Virginia.* 8th American ed. Boston: David Carlisle, 1801.

Johnston, Henry P. "Christian Febiger, Colonel of the Virginia Line of the Continental Army." *Magazine of American History* 6 (1881): 188–203.

————. *Yorktown Campaign*. New York: Harper & Bros., 1881.

Journal of the House of Delegates of Virginia. December 12, 1781. Richmond, VA: Thomas W. White, 1828.

Kimball, Marie Goebel. *Jefferson, War and Peace, 1776–1784*. New York: Coward-McCann, 1947.

King, Quentin Scott. *Henry Clay and the War of 1812*. Jefferson, NC: McFarland and Co., 2014.

Kranish, Michael. *Flight from Monticello: Thomas Jefferson at War*. New York: Oxford University Press, 2010.

Kukla, John. *Mister Jefferson's Women*. New York: Random House, 2008.

Lafayette, Marquis de. *Memoirs, Correspondence and Manuscripts of General Lafayette*. New York: Saunders and Otley, 1837.

Lafayette, Marquis de, to Thomas Nelson, June 28, 1781. Special Collections, John D. Rockefeller Jr. Library, Colonial Williamsburg Foundation, Williamsburg, VA. http://rocklib.omeka.net/items/show/472.

Lancaster, Alexander. *Historic Virginia Homes and Churches*. Philadelphia: J.B. Lippincott Company, 1915.

Lee, Henry. *Memoirs of the War in the Southern Department of the United States*. New York: New York Times Books, 1968 (reprint).

Lee, Nell Moore. *Patriot Above Profit*. Nashville, TN: Rutledge Hill Press, 1988.

Leepson, Marc. *Lafayette: Lessons in Leadership from the Idealist General*. New York: Palgrave Macmillan, 2011.

Leibiger, Stuart. "George Washington and Lafayette: Father and Son of the Revolution." In *Sons of the Father: George Washington and His Protégés*. Edited by Robert M.S. McDonald. Charlottesville: University of Virginia Press, 2013.

Lerche, Charles O., Jr. "Jefferson and the Election of 1800: A Case Study in the Political Smear." *William and Mary Quarterly*, 3rd ser., 5, no. 4 (October 1948): 467–91.

Lewis of Warner Hall. *The History of a Family, Including the Genealogy of Descendants in Both the Male and Female Lines*.... Baltimore, MD: Genealogical Publishing Co., 1935.

Lofaro, Michael. *Daniel Boone: An American Life*. Lexington: University Press of Kentucky, 2010.

Long, Stephen Meriwether. "British Lieutenant Colonel Banastre Tarleton and the American Revolution: Drama on the Plantations of Charlottesville." *Meriwether Connections* 24, no. 1 (January–March 2005) and no. 2 (April–June 2005).

Loth, Calder. *The Virginia Landmarks Register.* 4th ed. Charlottesville: University Press of Virginia, 1999.

Lounsbury, Carl. *The Courthouses of Early Virginia: An Architectural History.* Charlottesville: University of Virginia Press, 2005.

Lynch, Wayne. "Grading British General Benedict Arnold." *Journal of the American Revolution*, August 2, 2013. http://allthingsliberty.com/2013/08/grading-british-general-benedict-arnold.

Maass, John R. "The Greatest Terror Imaginable: Cornwallis Brings His Campaign to Goochland, June 1781." *Goochland County Historical Society Magazine* 41 (2009): 12–101.

———. "To Disturb the Assembly: Tarleton's Charlottesville Raid and the British Invasion of Virginia, 1781." *Virginia Cavalcade* 49 (Autumn 2000): 148–57.

Mack, Ebenezer. *The Life of Gilbert Motier de Lafayette…From Numerous and Authentic Sources.* 2nd ed. Ithaca, NY: Andrus, Woodruff & Gauntlett, 1843.

MacMaster, Richard, ed. "News of the Yorktown Campaign: The Journal of Dr. Robert Honyman, April 17–November 25, 1781." *Virginia Magazine of History and Biography* 79 (1971): 401–2.

Malone, Dumas. *Jefferson, the Virginian.* Boston: Little, Brown, 1948.

Mansfield, James R. *A History of Early Spotsylvania.* Orange, VA: Green Publishers, 1977.

Mapp, Alf J., Jr. *Thomas Jefferson: America's Paradoxical Patriot.* Lanham, MD: Rowman & Littlefield, 1987.

Martin, Peter. *Pleasure Gardens of Virginia: From Jamestown to Jefferson.* Charlottesville: University of Virginia Press, 2001.

McAllister, J.T. *Virginia Militia in the Revolution.* Hot Springs, VA: McAllister Publishing Co., 1913.

McDonnell, Michael A. *The Politics of War: Race, Class, and Conflict in Revolutionary Virginia.* Chapel Hill: University of North Carolina Press, 2007.

Merrill, Boynton. *Jefferson's Nephews: A Frontier Tragedy.* Princeton, NJ: Princeton University Press, 1976.

Mitchell, Samuel, and Margaret C. Mitchell. Revolutionary War Pension Application, W3851, January 28, 1833. http://www.revwarapps.org.

Morrissey, Brendan. *Yorktown 1781: The World Turned Upside Down.* London: Osprey, 1997.

"Mount Bernard Complex." National Register of Historic Places Registration Form, 2004. http://www.dhr.virginia.gov/registers/Counties/Goochland/037-0038_Mount_Bernard_Complex_2005_Final_Nomination.pdf.

Nash, Gary B. *The Unknown American Revolution: The Unruly Birth of Democracy and the Struggle to Create America*. New York: Penguin, 2005.

Nelson, James L. *George Washington's Great Gamble and the Sea Battle That Won the American Revolution*. New York: McGraw Hill, 2010.

Nelson, John. Revolutionary War Pension Application, W5414, January 9, 1827. http://www.revwarapps.org.

Nelson, Paul D. *Anthony Wayne: Soldier of the Early Republic*. Bloomington: Indiana University Press, 1985.

O'Shaughnessy, Andrew J. *The Men Who Lost America: British Leadership, the American Revolution, and the Fate of the Empire*. New Haven, CT: Yale University Press, 2013.

Palmer, William, ed. *Calendar of State Papers*. 2 vols. Richmond, VA: James E. Goode, 1881.

Pancake, John S. *This Destructive War: The British Campaign in the Carolinas, 1780–1782*. Tuscaloosa: University of Alabama Press, 1985.

Papageorgiou, Lizbeth Ward. *The Colonial Churches of St. Thomas' Parish, Orange County, Virginia*. Baltimore, MD: Genealogical Publishing Co., 2008.

Parton, James. *Life of Thomas Jefferson, Third President of the United States*. Boston: James R. Osgood, 1874.

"Peter Francisco, American Soldier." *William and Mary Quarterly*, 1st ser., 13, no. 4 (April 1905): 213–19.

Peterson, Merrill D. *Thomas Jefferson and the New Nation: A Biography*. New York: Oxford University Press, 1970.

Pybus, Cassandra. "Jefferson's Faulty Math: The Question of Slave Defections in the American Revolution." *William and Mary Quarterly*, 3rd ser., 62, no. 2 (April 2005): 243–64.

Quenzel, Carroll H. *The History and Background of St. George's Episcopal Church, Fredericksburg, Virginia*. Richmond: Saunders & Son, 1951.

Rainey, Peter G. *Germanna Road: Three Hundred Year History of Lower Orange County, Virginia*. Bloomington, IN: Author House, 2010.

Randall, Henry S. *The Life of Thomas Jefferson*. 3 vols. New York, Derby & Jackson, 1858.

Rice, Howard C., Jr., and Anne S.K. Brown, trans. and eds. *The American Campaigns of Rochambeau's Army, 1780, 1781, 1782, 1783*. 2 vols. Princeton, NJ: Princeton University Press, 1972.

Ross, Charles, ed. *Correspondence of Charles, First Marquis Cornwallis*. 2nd ed. 3 vols. London: John Murray, 1859.

Russell, T. Triplett. *Fauquier County in the Revolution*. Warrenton, VA: Fauquier County American Bicentennial Commission, 1976.

Saberton, Ian, ed. *The Cornwallis Papers: The Campaigns of 1780 and 1781 in the Southern Theatre of the American Revolutionary War*. 6 vols. East Sussex, UK: Naval & Military Press, 2010.

Selby, John. *Revolution in Virginia, 1775–1783*. Williamsburg, VA: Colonial Williamsburg Foundation, 1988.

Selig, Robert. *March to Victory: Washington, Rochambeau, and the Yorktown Campaign of 1781*. Washington, D.C.: U.S. Army Center of Military History, n.d.

Shepard, E. Lee, ed. *Marching to Victory: Captain Benjamin Bartholomew's Diary of the Yorktown Campaign, May 1781 to March 1782*. Richmond: Virginia Historical Society, 2002.

Simcoe, John Graves. *Simcoe's Military Journal: A History of the Operations of a Partisan Corps....* New York: Bartlett & Welford, 1844.

Slaughter, Philip. *A History of St. Mark's Parish, Culpeper County, Virginia*. Baltimore, MD: Innes and Co., 1877.

Smith, Paul H., ed. *Letters of Delegates to Congress, 1774–1789*. 26 vols. Washington, D.C.: Library of Congress, 1976–2000.

Stedman, Charles. *History of the Origin, Progress, and Termination of the American War*. 2 vols. London: J. Murray, 1794.

Syrett, Harold C., ed. *The Papers of Alexander Hamilton*. 27 vols. New York: Columbia University Press, 1961–87.

Tarleton, Banastre. *A History of the Campaigns of 1780 and 1781 in the Southern Provinces of North America*. Dublin: Colles, Exshaw, White, 1787.

Taylor, Alan. *The Internal Enemy: Slavery and War in Virginia, 1772–1832*. New York: W.W. Norton, 2013.

Thomas Jefferson Papers. Ser. 1, General Correspondence, 1651–1827. American Memory Collection. Library of Congress, http://memory.loc.gov/ammem/collections/jefferson_papers.

Toler, John. "Remembering Red House, the Skinner Family, and Early Haymarket." *Haymarket Lifestyle* (September 2010): 8–9.

Tower, Charlemagne. *The Marquis de La Fayette in the American Revolution*. 2 vols. Philadelphia: J.B. Lippincott Company, 1890.

Trussell, John B.B. *The Pennsylvania Line: Regimental Organization and Operations, 1775–1783*. Harrisburg: Pennsylvania Historical and Museum Commission, 1993.

Tucker, Glenn. *Mad Anthony Wayne and the New Nation*. Harrisburg, PA: Stackpole Books, 1973.

Urwin, Gregory J. "Cornwallis and the Slaves of Virginia: A New Look at the Yorktown Campaign." In *Coming to the Americas: The Eurasian Military Impact on the Development of the Western Hemisphere*. Edited by John A. Lynn.

Wheaton, IL: Cantigny First Division Foundation for the United States Commission on Military History, 2003.

————. "When Freedom Wore a Red Coat: How Cornwallis' 1781 Campaign Threatened the Revolution in Virginia." *Army History* (Summer 2008): 6–23.

Virginia Conservation Commission. *Virginia: A Guide to the Old Dominion.* 6th ed. Richmond: James H. Price, governor, 1956.

Virginia Gazette. November 14, 1751; March 23, 1775.

Voorhis, Manning C. "Bollingbrook." *William and Mary Quarterly*, 2nd ser., 16, no. 4 (October 1936): 545–53.

Waddell, Joseph, ed. "Diary of Captain John Davis of the Pennsylvania Line." *Virginia Magazine of History and Biography* 1, no. 1 (July 1893): 1–16.

Ward, Christopher. *War of the Revolution.* 2 vols. New York: Macmillan, 1952.

Ward, Harry M., and Harold E. Greer. *Richmond During the Revolution, 1775–1783.* Charlottesville: University Press of Virginia, 1977.

Washington, H.A., ed. *The Writings of Thomas Jefferson.* 9 vols. New York: John C. Riker, 1853.

Weeks, Ellie. "Thomas Jefferson's Elk-Hill." *Goochland County Historical Society Magazine* 3, no. 1 (n.d.): 6.

Weigley, Russell F. *An American Way of War: A History of United States Military Strategy and Power.* New York: Macmillan, 1973.

————. *Towards an American Army: Military Thought from Washington to Marshall.* New York: Columbia University Press, 1962.

Wickwire, Franklin, and Mary Wickwire. *Cornwallis: The American Adventure.* Boston: Houghton Mifflin, 1970.

Willcox, William B. "British Road to Yorktown: A Study in Divided Command." *William and Mary Quarterly*, 3rd ser., 52, no. 1 (October 1946): 1–35.

Wilson, Gaye. "A Narrow Escape from the British, Thanks to Jack Jouett." *Monticello Newsletter* 17 (Winter 2006).

Wright, John W. "The Corps of Light Infantry in the Continental Army." *American Historical Review* 31, no. 3 (April 1926): 454–61.

Wright, Robert K. *The Continental Army.* Washington, D.C.: U.S. Army Center of Military History, 1983.

Wyllie, John Cooke. *Daniel Boone's Adventures in Charlottesville in 1781; Some Incidents Connected with Tarleton's Raid.* Charlottesville, VA: Albemarle County Historical Society, 1963.

INDEX

ABOUT THE AUTHOR

John R. Maass received a BA in history from Washington and Lee University, an MA in U.S. history from the University of North Carolina–Greensboro and a PhD in early American history from Ohio State University. He is a historian at the U.S. Army Center of Military History in Washington, D.C. His publications include *North Carolina and the French and Indian War: The Spreading Flames of War* (The History Press, 2013) and *Defending a New Nation, 1783–1811* in the U.S. Army Campaigns of the War of 1812 Series (U.S. Army, 2013). He was an officer in the U.S. Army Reserves and past president and founder of the Rockbridge Civil War Roundtable. He has contributed scholarly articles to *The Journal of Military History*, *Virginia Cavalcade*, *Army History*, *The Journal of Backcountry Studies* and *The North Carolina Historical Review*. He lives with his family in the Mount Vernon area of Fairfax County, Virginia.